SOMBREROS ARE BECOMING

by

Nancy Johnstone

The Clapton Press

First published by Faber & Faber Limited, 1941

This edition © 2023 The Clapton Press Limited

Cover design by Gruffydd Art

ISBN 978-1-913693-27-5

The Clapton Press Limited
38 Thistlewaite Road
London E5 0QQ

About the Author

Bored with life in Fleet Street, Nancy and Archie Johnstone left their jobs and moved to the Costa Brava in 1934 to build and run their own hotel. Within twelve months Tossa de Mar became the destination of choice for a vibrant group of international writers and artists. The first volume of Nancy's memoir, *Hotel in Spain,* is a light-hearted account of their ups and downs before the Civil War erupted and darkness descended.

Her sequel, *Hotel in Flight*—also available from The Clapton Press—continues their story after the couple refuse an offer of evacuation from the Royal Navy and convert their hotel into a refuge for children displaced by the war, eventually escorting them in a terrifying dash for the border as Franco's mercenary army bombed and shelled its way to Barcelona. The children were immediately interned in a French concentration camp.

The Johnstones emigrated to Mexico in 1939, leaving nearly all their possessions behind them. *Sombreros Are Becoming* is the third and final volume of Nancy's memoirs, another light-hearted narrative recounting their journey to Mexico and the experience of rebuilding their lives in Cuernavaca.

They later went their separate ways. Archie defected to the Soviet Union in 1947, where he died in 1963. In January 1951, Nancy was seriously injured in a car crash in Guatemala in which her friend, the former head of the Spanish Republic's Foreign Press Office, Constancia de la Mora, was killed. The same year she sold the hotel in Tossa de Mar and wrote to her publisher leaving a forwarding address; she was never heard from again.

George Nichols

Contents

1 – Travelling Light 7
2 – Untamed Lion 18
3 – The Man Who Wasn't There . . . 25
4 – Goodbye to the Children 33
5 – Old Man in the Closet 40
6 – Once in Mexico 47
7 – Street Car Frolics 56
8 – Typical Tropical Trips 65
9 – Everybody Gets Everything 74
10 – Mean Altitude 81
11 – Wrong Side of the *Barranca* . . . 88
12 – Living on $28 a Month 96
13 – A Drumming Noise 106
14 – Scorpions and *Pulque* 112
15 – Neighbours, Just Neighbours . . . 121
16 – Moustache in the Sun 130
17 – Geese and Irrigation 139
18 – Chorus of Space-Sellers 148
19 – Soul of a Bank 157
20 – Nest of International Spies . . . 167
21 – Life in the *Quinta* 176

22 – She Calls Herself Alhambra. . . .	185
23 – Jack Has Some Gossip	191
24 – Pride of the Penitentiary	199
25 – Life, Death and Terry	207
26 – You Can Lead a Steamroller to Water .	217
27 – Stocktaking	227

Chapter 1
Travelling Light

'Hi! Take this,' shouted Archie. 'Run for the train while I get the tickets.'

I grabbed the suitcase and the rucksack, picked up the smaller suitcase and my typewriter in the other hand, and sprinted across the rails. Porters yelled at me in Marseillais French; bells rang; loudspeakers boomed. Marseilles station seemed enormous in the half light as I made for the Nice express. I staggered into a compartment just as Archie came up with the tickets. The train pulled out as we collapsed in our seats.

Archie was busy counting his change and sorting out his French notes. I looked at the heap of luggage on the floor: one small suitcase, one larger suitcase, an old rucksack, and the typewriter.

'Archie,' I said suddenly. 'Do you realize I have carried alone across Marseilles station every possession we have in the world?'

'There is something satisfactory about being able to carry all one's possessions single-handed,' said Archie.

'Especially if *I* do the carrying,' I remarked. 'When we go to Mexico—'

'Are we going to Mexico?'

'Of course we are going to Mexico. Where else can we go?'

'I've always liked the idea of Mexico,' said Archie thoughtfully.

'I haven't,' I said. 'I have never hankered after the tropics. But at least the Mexican Government was swell over Spain.'

'There is the question of money,' began Archie.

'Oh, money!' I said.

When we left Catalunya, Spain, on the 10th of February 1939, we left in company with about 500,000 refugees. Of these, seventy children were directly in our charge. We had left our home in Tossa de Mar, a little seaside village a hundred miles from the French border, where we had turned what used to be our thriving hotel, the Casa Johnstone, into a refugee children's colony. We left because it did not seem a good idea to leave children to the mercy of light-hearted machine-gunners in airplanes (Tossa was machine-gunned two days before we left) or to the exuberant spirits of victorious Moors who invariably formed the vanguard of Franco's forces when entering villages. We also left because we, too, did not care for machine-guns and Moors.

We knew what we were doing. We were leaving our property, all our possessions except what we could carry, our small black Pekinese, Beetle, and our very dear Francisca, who had worked with us before and during the Spanish war. We were also leaving the place we considered our home and some of our best friends. We were leaving in company with thousands of children; thousands of Republicans who had always been loyal to their country; thousands of people who had no idea of politics but who were just plain scared; thousands of intellectuals; the International Brigades who had been withdrawn from the front some months earlier as a gesture by Negrín; and, fighting a rearguard action to allow us all to escape into France, the cream of the Spanish Republican army.

We knew what we might expect: probably to lose our property and everything we had left in Spain. We had no money outside. We had two suitcases, a rucksack and a typewriter.

In Perpignan we worked in the concentration camps with the Quaker Relief Organisation. Our own small affairs seemed infinitessimal beside the colossal tragedy of the refugees. We worked frantically so as not to have time to think. We had no idea where our refugee children had been sent by the French authorities. We knew that Tossa had been taken by the Fascist troops shortly after we left.

Archie and I seldom met. We shared with anybody any bed we could find. Perpignan was packed with refugees and relief workers. A tall, well-dressed English woman called Margaret Travers offered me half a bed. She had come up from the South of France, where she was on vacation, to help the refugees. She came in a car with an incoherent but charming Portuguese boy to drive it. The Portuguese boy was willing to drive anything at any time anywhere. He was commandeered for relief lorries; sent off to lonely waits in the mountains while committees changed their minds about loads of bread and forgot about him; dragged out of bed (which he shared with three refugees) to change tyres or patch up engines. He never lost his temper and invariably smiled at everyone.

Archie and I earned a few pounds writing for the English press; I, as usual, working hard at articles for the *Manchester Guardian* and getting paid half of Archie's earnings from things he rushed off for his old newspaper, the *News Chronicle*. People we had helped in the days when we were rich in Spain suddenly turned up and returned sums we had never even considered as loans. With our earnings and unexpected repayments we found we had about fifty pounds. With that and the typewriter we were well off.

It simply never struck either of us to return to England. Archie was always certain of a newspaper job in London because he had a name for being—among other things, of course—reliable and sober. Our British passports were in order. But the British role in the Spanish war made the thought of returning there out of the question. Besides, we did not like the climate.

We discussed where we should go. The need for us as relief workers was diminishing, not because less relief was needed, but funds were getting low. The remaining work was for experts like Audrey Russell, Donald Darling and Richard Rees, who could deal with committees and their idiosyncrasies. One charming incident cheered us. A British general had been sent from the War Office to check the withdrawal of the International Brigades. One of his duties was to locate the British members and to send them home. He was so impressed by the wonderful aspect of the Brigades and he sent back such glowing reports to the War Office as to the excellence of the men that the War Office recalled him. It would never do to have a general getting lyrical about 'Reds'. The General blew through his moustache and snorted what he thought of the War Office. Then he stayed on in Perpignan and joined the relief workers. 'Damn me, can't let a fine set of men starve, by gad. What England needs today . . .'

The Johnstone luck asserted itself. Margaret Travers, whose bed I had gratefully shared whenever it was not too full of refugees, suggested that we come back with her in her car to Saint-Raphael, where she and her mother had rented a villa. There we could have a much needed rest, I could decide on my next book, Archie could write newspaper articles and, best of all, we could actually have breakfast in bed. And a bed, a whole bed with sheets and everything! It sounded like a dream. We had not slept in a real bed, that is to say a bed without two or three others in it, for four weeks. Before that, we had not even seen a bed or taken off our clothes for twelve days.

We started off in Margaret's car, driven by João, the Portuguese boy. It was March, a mild, sunny March, luckily for those cooped up in the concentration camps. We determined to get our minds off the appalling tragedy and as we went further into France the tragedy did not bulk so large. Our escape mechanism began to work; we began to think about ourselves. We bought French cheeses and crisp bread and had a picnic outside Nîmes. We were near Tarascon and I was dreaming of my schooldays, when we struggled through Daudet's Tartarin de Tarascon, when the car gave a gentle sigh and stopped.

João was efficient, but even he could do nothing about a broken shaft. We eventually saw a car approaching down the country road. It was the first car for hours, but it had a bright young man who went in for mountain climbing and he had his rope with him. He towed us to Istre, where we left the car in a garage in the charge of João, who seemed perfectly happy to remain a night in Istre. We left him talking incomprehensible French to two polite young air force officers.

Margaret decided to take the next bus to Marseilles and to get the train from there. We loved Istre and waited until a later bus, which allowed us three minutes to catch the train. We caught it. And I carried everything we owned across Marseilles station all by myself—a small suitcase, a larger suitcase, a rucksack and a typewriter.

The first few days at Saint-Raphael were wrapped in a haze of contentment. We lay in bed until noon, gazing out of the window at the sweep of the bay. We relaxed utterly, and consequently realized how tired we were. The Travers family was perfect. Margaret appeared just at the right moments with books, Mrs Travers was undismayed at having total strangers thrust on her, Mrs Newell, the housekeeper, spoiled us completely. We had a wonderful time. We were in danger of forgetting that we were Archie and Nancy Johnstone, around whom life cannot flow smoothly for long, except for one little incident which happened soon after our arrival.

We had managed to pull ourselves together sufficiently to come down to the drawing-room for tea. We toasted our feet before a log fire and ate English muffins to Mrs Travers' witty conversation. Presently Mrs Newell announced a visitor.

A distraught female swept into the room in a large black hat.

'And what have you done with my son?' demanded the figure which seemed to be about six feet tall.

'Your son?' we echoed blankly.

Mrs Travers smiled calmly. 'Don't get so excited, Francesca,' she said mildly. 'João is perfectly all right. *He* stayed with the car at Istre.'

The black hat quivered dangerously.

'The idea of leaving him alone in Istre! Of course he will *be* in prison by this time.'

What a crazy woman, I thought. People were always *getting* picked *up* by the police in *Perpignan* in the general hysteria—actually João was one of the few foreigners in Perpignan who was *never* arrested—but it was ridiculous to *get* so worked up just because the young man had stayed behind to see to the car. He seemed perfectly well able to look after himself.

'I don't see what can happen to him at Istre,' I ventured. 'After all, it is miles from the frontier, where things are really difficult.'

The black hat swept round at me.

'You don't know anything,' declared Francesca. 'João always gets mixed up with the police. After all, he's my adopted son. I ought to know.'

Mrs Travers seemed to be used to the lady. She talked in her calm way and almost succeeded in persuading her that perhaps nothing might happen to João in Istre. Then the telephone rang. Francesca sat up with a start.

'There!' she said.

She dashed out into the hall and snatched the telephone. Presently she came back.

'Of course, he's in trouble with the police.' she said, and strangely enough was perfectly calm now that she knew the worst. 'I shall leave immediately for Istre. It's very inconvenient.' She looked severely at us and we felt terribly guilty to think we had for a moment thought that João would be safe at Istre, or for that matter anywhere else.

'Can we do anything to help?' we asked humbly.

'Oh, I shall get him out in no time,' she said, now perfectly cheerful. 'I have all our papers in order and it's just a matter of going there and talking to the police.'

'Why did they arrest him?' we ventured to ask.

She stood in the doorway, the top of the hat just touching the lintel. She was no longer distraught and looked very handsome and smart in her black suit.

'Oh!' she said with a smile. 'He was exploring the airfield. You know how suspicious the French are!'

We have since seen Francesca in many situations and I

am sure it is years since she has worn a hat, but I shall never forget my first impression of her in Mrs Newell's drawing-room in Saint-Raphael.

Saint-Raphael seemed heaven to us but it is really a terrible place. In the winter it is the haven of all the aged British who feel that Nice is vulgar and Monte Carlo fast. Why they travel all the way from England to meet the bitter blast of the *mistral* which sweeps almost continually across the gulf of Fréjus is a mystery, but I admit I have not spent a winter in England in years. The Travers came to Saint-Raphael in ignorance of the climate and it must be admitted that Mr Maplethorpe, housing and estate agent, did much to compensate for the *mistral*.

Mr Maplethorpe, a soft-spoken, slightly bald, plumpish Britisher, lived in Saint-Raphael with his French wife. We heard about him long before we met him.

'My dear, ask Mr Maplethorpe—'

'Mr Maplethorpe with be sure to know.'

'Of course Mr Maplethorpe will change your cheque, lend you books, change pound notes, fix up your permit to stay, find you a house, sell you a house, lend you his car, take you anywhere, find you a lawyer, do anything.'

When we met him we told him we had been in the hotel business. We also told him we appreciated his publicity sense. He smiled: 'I find doing small favours for clients worth pounds in advertising,' he said as he drove us to the next town to get our papers fixed.

Margaret Travers had collected funds in aid of the Spanish refugees. It took some doing in Saint-Raphael. Most of the foreigners were still at the stage where they supposed Franco must be all right because he was a gentleman. Margaret and a few long-suffering friends were cut at the Golf Club, sniffed at over bridge tables and would have been ostracized entirely except for the fact that Margaret was so utterly 'British County' in her appearance. A small group of sympathizers invited her to come to the Grand Hotel on her return from Perpignan to tell them about the refugees. They were delighted when she said she could actually bring two refugees, quite nice clean ones who spoke English. Archie and I felt anything we could do would ease our consciences when we compared our lot with that of most of our friends. We agreed to go with Margaret to the Grand Hotel.

Archie and I had been five years in Spain. We had stayed there throughout the Spanish war except for a three month interval in England in the summer of 1938. There is no doubt that we had picked up some odd habits during the war. We were inclined to pocket any bread left over at meals to do for the next meal; we saved cigarette stubs in order to unravel them to roll up again into cigarettes; we had no respect for public or private buildings. That is to say, we felt that, given a number of homeless children, any available shelter should be utilized. We had got a bad habit of calling facts by their real names, and after the harsh realities of bombardments and air raids we had forgotten all the conversation and window-dressing necessary to the more civilized. Among other things, we had forgotten that people 'dressed' in the evening.

We might have remembered if we had been in Antibes, which has some pretensions to being gay, but Saint-Raphael went dead after dark. So Archie, in his corduroy trousers and aged leather jacket and I, most conventional in a tweed skirt and woollen sweater, went solemnly up to the Grand Hotel at 9.00 pm. Margaret Travers basely deserted us at the last moment, saying she had a headache.

The Grand Hotel seemed ghostly. There was one dim

light in the entrance hall and a sleepy hall-porter seemed amazed to see us. He reluctantly ushered us into a vast room plunged into gloom except for two small lights over some tables in a corner. At the tables, in somnolent state, sat fifteen people in full evening dress.

'We were just going to bed,' said a petulant voice out of the gloom. Something white fluttered and I saw it was a parson's collar.

'Well, never mind,' said one good-hearted American woman. 'Come right over here, Miss Travers, and sit at the head of the party. We are so interested to know just how you used the funds.'

'I'm sorry,' I said. 'I'm not Miss Travers. I only came there tonight because she thought you might all be interested to talk to someone from Spain. My husband and I lived there.'

'How like Margaret,' said someone else. 'And we have all waited here to hear about the accounts.'

There was some conversation about Margaret. So unconventional, charming of course, but one simply never knew where one was . . .

'Let's get out of here,' I whispered to Archie.

'No you don't,' he said. 'You go right in there and do your stuff.'

'We might at least get some coffee out of them,' I said.

'Well—ah—Mrs—ah—Johnson,' boomed the parson. 'Very interesting, I'm sure. Quite an experience.'

'Oh dear,' said one woman. 'I'm afraid we can't offer you coffee. The staff have gone to the movies at Fréjus.'

'I didn't come here to drink coffee,' I lied. 'I came to talk about Spain and the refugees. I won't keep you long out of your beds.'

I talked. I threw it at them in chunks. I fairly stunned

them with details of the great retreat. I could see Archie hugging himself. Every now and then he would interrupt me with a quiet, 'My wife is rather understating there. It is 40 per cent of the wounded who are dying in the camps for lack of treatment.' Or, 'Just a minute—don't exaggerate. There were only four thousand men penned into that football field, not five thousand.'

It got them. Even the parson was silent. The kind American woman was in tears. We left them sitting quietly in the gloom in their evening clothes. We certainly spoiled their sleep.

The next day I met one of the group as I walked through the town. She came up with tremendous enthusiasm. 'Mrs Johnstone, how too stupid of me last night. Of course, I didn't know then that you were an author.'

Chapter 2
Untamed Lion

For a while I was a sort of untamed lion in Saint-Raphael. Untamed, because I would not jump through the hoops so temptingly held out for me. It appears that very few authors ever come to Saint-Raphael. However, I was too soon utterly eclipsed.

We decided that we would rent a small villa on the sea while I wrote *Hotel in Flight,* which my London publishers were demanding. Rents were surprisingly cheap and the cost of living reasonable. We found the top storey of a large villa right on the cliff was for rent for about twelve dollars a month. It had a bedroom and a sitting-room opening out on an enormous sun terrace, a kitchen and even a bathroom with a geyser. The terrace had a ship's ladder which led up to another terrace with one big studio room, the top of which was yet another terrace. We could look over the pine vista of Fréjus bay right across to Saint-Tropez, that is when it was possible to see anything with eyes streaming in the wind. The owners of the villa lived down below.

While we were choosing our villa, Richard Rees of the International Relief Commission arrived. He was utterly exhausted after months of ambulance driving in Spain and then months of working in the concentration camps. He immediately decided to stay in Saint-Raphael, and he rented a villa near ours. He told us that he was expecting a friend called Mark Benney to share the villa with him. It was this Mark Benney who put me as an author utterly in the shade. He had written a best seller, *Angels in Undress.*

He had been serialized in the London *Evening News*. He was a personal friend of H G Wells. He was *someone*.

He certainly was. He was a deceptively shy-looking little man with a peculiar prison pallor. One almost expected him to speak out of the side of his mouth. He nearly did. The Britishers in Saint-Raphael eagerly ordered his book from the obliging Mr Maplethorpe. There was a sort of breathless hush while dozens of rheumatic fingers wrestled with the pages of *Angels in Undress*. There was an almost audible gasp when the contents of the book were grasped. There was no getting away from it. Mark Benney was a jailbird.

Mark Benney used to be a burglar. He was a remarkably bad burglar. Life has its compensations and many prison sentences enabled Mark to study in the prison libraries. I would like to think that the British prison system is such that it could turn out writers like Mark, but I am afraid that Mark happens to be a singularly gifted person. As a burglar he is a wash-out. As a writer he is very near genius. In *Angels of Undress* he tells the story of his childhood in Soho; his attempts at burglary, which he takes very seriously; his old reform school days at Borstal; his love affairs; his philosophy of life. The Britishers of Saint-Raphael read his book and then looked under their beds every night.

The Golf Club was in a dilemma about Mark. As a famous author he should have been welcome around that august fireplace; as a burglar he was obviously out of place. It was a difficult situation. Mark himself settled it. He and Richard and I went for a long tramp over the Esterel mountains behind Saint-Raphael and fetched up at the Golf Club for tea. We walked in wearing very old flannel trousers, dilapidated sand-shoes, and no socks. The Golf

Club decided that Mark was pure Borstal. They did not know that Sir Richard Rees, Bart, was pure Eton.

It was interesting to hear Mark and Richard discussing their old schools. It seems that Borstal is run exactly on the same lines of England's most famous public school. Public school is a kind of English joke. There is nothing so private as the English public school, the least expensive of which charges about £150 a year to underfeed a boy and turns him out to be an English gentleman. Borstal and Eton have the same slang, the same institutions, and much the same food, but the Borstal boy usually ends up in prison and the Eton boy in the Cabinet.

If the Britishers of Saint-Raphael were puzzled whether to treat Mark as an author or as a burglar, there was no doubt which Mark considered to be the more important. It seemed strange that a man with so little talent for burglary should be so anxious to be a good burglar. He admitted that he really had not the temperament a first-class burglar required. Mark, having by some miracle effected an entry into a house, would often find himself paying far more attention to the owner's books, or to some aesthetically perfect but financially unsound picture or ornament, than to the professional burglar's standby, the family silver. The truth was that Mark was always an amateur in the burglary line, although he had every opportunity to be a professional. He was hurt if this was pointed out to him.

The only knowledge we had of Mark's burglariousness was from his book and his conversation. Mark never mixed his professions. In fact he admitted with some sadness that his burglaring days were over. He could not put his heart into it unless he was in need, and he admitted that he could earn far more as a writer than as a burglar. One had the feeling that Mark yearned a little for the good old days as he sat in his comfortable villa in Saint-Raphael among the waving pines. One night we were awakened by stones thrown at our bedroom window. It was Mark, wanting a bed for the night. He had lost the key of his villa and could not get in. We were the more convinced in our idea that Mark was a born writer.

We settled down in our villa. Not counting the fact that the daughter of the house played *Liebestraum* on the piano very badly every morning for an hour or two, there was peace except for occasional seaplanes roaring overhead. We ducked nervously at first but soon got used to them and the warships in the bay.

I was able to work very well in the big upstairs room. It was April 1939 and I had promised the finished manuscript by the first of June. I worked three hours in the mornings and then Archie and I usually took our lunch down to the beach. The water was still much too cold for bathing but the sun was hot when one could get out of the wind and the beach was sheltered. The coast was entirely unlike the Costa Brava in Catalunya where, to quote our hotel folder, the great *cliffs* cascade *down* to the sea in a series of giant rock gardens. On the Côte d'Azur the cliffs slope down gently to the bays and beaches and it is not surprising to find pine trees growing right out of the sand. The effect of trees almost in the sea is attractive. The whole coast is more tame and civilized than the wild Catalan coast and in some ways prettier. It is never a shock to find a golf course or a carefully laid-out park and neat, white villas with bougainvillea and mimosa fitting into the general sleekness.

Away from the coast, inland among the Esterel mountains, the atmosphere is different. Linen-clad visitors do not penetrate into the interior and there are the real

Provençal farms and the hardy Provençal people. Archie loathes walking—he gets mysterious aches in his back when anyone suggests a walk—but luckily Richard Rees could stride on for miles and he and I went for some wonderful tramps in search of rare wild flowers. We met and talked to farmers while we drank their wine and to goatherds perched on the peaks of the hills. They all wanted to ask us one thing. When was the war coming?

Everyone in and around Saint-Raphael talked about the war. Everyone in the whole of the South of France was wondering just when the Italians would try to take Nice. There was no hysteria, which was relief after the atmosphere in Perpignan, but the air seemed to vibrate with anxious question marks. The vegetable woman bringing round her hand-cart would tell how the rumble of special trains rushing guns and troops up to the Italian border had shaken her little hut by the railway line all night. Senegalese troops suddenly appeared to guard all the roads and bridges. Everyone was alarmed and they were still more alarmed when the Senegalese troops all disappeared as suddenly as they had arrived. What did it all mean? No one seemed to question for a moment that the war was coming. It was only a matter of time.

Archie and I had just had nearly three years of war in Spain, We felt we could not stand another. In Spain we had known what we were fighting for. The coming war looked to us as if the issues might be obscure. In any case we were tired. Archie was so tired that he sat all day in the sun and very slowly expanded to his normal size. He agreed with me that it was a good idea to get out of Europe but he could not make any effort about it.

Richard, Mark, Archie and I would discuss for hours the possibility or inevitability of war. We all agreed on the inevitability but we Estoril argued about the immediate danger.

'There have been so many scares,' said Mark.

'The situation is so precarious,' said Richard, 'that anything might start it off with a bang at any moment. Or it can hang on like this for another year.'

'I don't want to hang on and wait for it,' said Archie vaguely.

'We won't,' I said.

'Where will you go?' asked Mark. 'An island in the South Seas?'

Archie brightened. He has never outgrown the desire to live on an island in the South Seas.

'I shall try to get a job as an interpreter for the Spanish refugees,' said Richard. 'The French will want to use them if there's a war. It would be better than leaving them to rot in the camps.'

'I suppose I shall go back to England and join up,' said Mark thoughtfully. 'There's always something to be done somewhere.'

'Well, we're getting out,' I said.

'All right. Where to?'

'We're going to Mexico,' I said triumphantly.

'I still don't see what we're going to use for money,' said Archie mildly.

'That's not a bad idea,' said Mark. 'I wouldn't mind going to Mexico.'

'I've always wanted to go to Mexico,' said Archie. 'But I don't see how we're going to get there. It costs something to cross the Atlantic.'

'You leave it to me,' I said. 'You know what happens when I set my mind on anything.'

Archie thought of the days when he had been a peaceful

editor in Fleet Street. He thought how he had been uprooted from his newspaper office to the Costa Brava in Catalunya. He thought of how he learned to be a waiter, a hotel keeper and an excellent landscape gardener. Then he found himself being a war correspondent. Later he was a director of a refugee children's colony. Back to newspaper work mixed with relief work in Perpignan, he was now relaxing in the South of France. There would be nothing surprising about finding himself in Mexico.

Chapter 3
The Man Who Wasn't There

With my typewriter going full blast in the morning to the accompaniment of the daughter of the house on the piano, the villa rocked. Archie balanced serenely, knee-deep in maps.

When Archie is sold on the idea of going to a place, he likes to find out where it is. In no time at all he knows the exact location, the climate, the vegetation, the cost of living, the mineral content per cubic metre, the trend politically and a quantity of obscure information both historical and geographical. Then he finds out how to get there. Usually he discovers some unusual route but to get to México we only had one consideration—how to do it as cheaply as possible.

Francesca, the excited lady in the black hat and the adopted mother of the Portuguese boy, was rich in information. She knew all about third-class travel and did not disguise the fact that it could be extremely uncomfortable. We had an idea that we could save money by getting a boat from Marseilles. We wrote to all the steamship companies that seemed possible and to the Mexican Consulate in London. Francesca was interested in our plans. She said she might almost come with us. We said politely it would be fine but we feared João with his penchant for arousing the worst in policemen might find the Mexican worst worse than the French worst.

We wrote to our friends in England telling them we were going to Mexico. Our conservative friends regretted that

Mexico was so far and were convinced that we were plunging into more civil wars; our more broad-minded friends all said they wished to come with us. Our refugee friends, who had no papers and were unable to move from wherever they had drifted, all congratulated us on our luck to be able to get out and several of them returned sums of money we had lent them. An old friend of my family gave me fifty pounds with his blessing; Archie's 85-year-old mother sent him ten pounds; another friend lent us forty pounds; my three slightly disapproving aunts produced thirty pounds between them and my London publishers nobly came across with an advance before they had the manuscript. We seemed all set to go.

The Mexican consul in London referred us to the Mexican Embassy in Paris. Mexico had broken off diplomatic relations with England over the oil controversy. We had heard the news in Spain and it had brightened us for days. The Mexican Embassy in Paris sent us a book of rules for getting into Mexico. It seemed that Mexico was not wanting foreigners from Europe. There was a variety of complicated documents to be obtained and we were expected to put down the equivalent of £35 each as a guaranty before we would be allowed to set foot ashore. The idea of tying up £70 of our small amount of money was a blow. Both Archie and I felt we could be earning enough in six months to keep us in any country, but we liked to feel that we had enough actual cash to cover six months. It was clear to us that there was nowhere to stay in Europe. We found several English people in Saint-Raphael who could not understand this. They agreed that a war must come and they did not want to go to England but they thought they would be quite all right in Greece.

'But Italy has just taken Albania,' we exclaimed. 'That

means Greece is bound to be involved.'

Those who agreed that the Balkans were not noted for their peacefulness thought that Portugal or Spain would be out of the next war. They dismissed our contention that Spain was a colony of Hitler's.

'Oh, you're prejudiced,' they said. 'Of course, after being in that war and everything. But you'll see. Franco needs money. He'll have to turn to England for that.'

We disagreed and decided to get out. The United States was too expensive; the USSR was too cold; South America was too problematical; we did not consider a British colony because we preferred to disassociate ourselves from the British Government. Mexico seemed indicated. It was a pity that we would have to tie up so much of our capital to be allowed in, but we could not grumble. We were better off than our refugee friends.

All this time we had not heard a word from our refugee children. We tried various ways to get in touch with them but all the refugee organizations were working overtime trying to get families in touch with one another. At last we got a letter from Leonor, the Aragonese woman in charge of the children, written by her small daughter Angelines. Our children were still together under her care and they were all in Besançon, near the Swiss border. They were in a convent and being well fed, although some of the older children were scared because of their experiences in schools in Spain before the war. They were afraid they would not be allowed to have proper lessons, but these French nuns treated the children extremely well and no-one had to go to Mass unless they wanted to.

We were thrilled to hear from our children. We wrote to them and told them we would come to see them just as soon as we could manage it. We wanted to dash off to

Besançon immediately but the expense stopped us. We were living as economically as possible to save up every cent for Mexico and a journey across France could not be undertaken lightly.

Living was cheap. We found that we could live well on a pound a week. Our total expenses for a month were usually eight or nine pounds. This included a few necessities such as trousers for Archie, material for cotton frocks for me, espadrilles, and an occasional drink in a café. But we had to cut out the usual life of Saint-Raphael altogether. We did not mind this, because it was dull. After lunch on the beach or, if the wind was blowing the wrong way, in a sheltered spot in the hinterland, we rested an hour or so in the sunshine. Then we would go back to the villa and I would work my second three hours, finishing my chapter for the day. After tea we usually went for a walk or played the native game of *boules* in the local inn. This is a speciality of Provence, placed with heavy metal balls on a sandy space. Someone throws a small wooden jack in any direction he likes and the idea is for the others to roll up their *boules* as near to it as possible. The French get tremendously excited about it and Archie, Richard and Mark liked the game. I found it tedious, but I was always perfectly happy to sit, with my knitting and a glass of vermouth, to watch. I liked to be among the local people, who were charmingly good-natured and gay. Richard and Mark usually came back to supper with us and the rest of the evening was spent in listening to the erudite arguments of the three of them. Archie could hold his own with them but I was not in that class.

Richard was suffering from a peculiar circumstance which seemed devoid of solution. He found that he was not in France at all. The rest of us had all been to get our identity cards arranged because to be anywhere in Europe at that time without all one's many papers in order meant endless trouble and probably prison. It never struck the authorities that the only people likely to have all their papers perfect were the spies and counterspies. It was dangerous to leave your house without passports and identity cards in case a policeman took it into his head to question you. So we paid our money for the necessary stamps, interviewed officials and gained little grey-blue cards containing photographs in profile showing the right ear. The French considered the ear the surest identification.

Richard went to get his card in all innocence of the fact that he was not really there at all. The officials thought he was there and greeted him amicably until they looked at his passport. There was no stamp to show that he had entered France. *Eh bien, voyons, il n'est pas ici!*

When we crossed the border into France with our children we had actually been included in a collective passport covering seventy odd of us. But for some reason I had taken Archie's and my passports to a little shack where a French official had stamped them with a date of our entry into France. It was pure chance that I had done so and Richard, running in and out of Spain with a special pass of the relief organization, had never noticed or thought about the official or about his passport.

It was difficult. What with the Italians massing on the border, refugees over-running the countryside and now a man who said he was there and who obviously could not be in France at all—the officials were in a dilemma. The could not admit it was the fault of their official at the border and if Richard had really tried to put something over, he should go to jail. All foreigners were heavily suspect.

They declined to give him a card for the moment and warned him that he must not consider for one minute that he was in France until he did get his card. He got it eventually but they managed to slip in a little clause saying that as the holder had not entered France he could not get the special reduction on railroads accorded to all holders of tourist cards.

Mark went back to London to be there for the publication of his latest book; he was thinking seriously of following our example and of coming to Mexico. Richard went back to Perpignan to take up his work again among the refugees. He was determined to stay for any war that might eventually materialize and to try to pick up the pieces. He did not think war was imminent. We went on with our preparations to leave.

Once we had decided to go to Mexico and it seemed to be possible, I was in a panic to be off. I had an awful feeling that by not making every effort to get away soon, we might never get away. Archie was curiously indifferent about being caught in a war. He was more interested in the fact that we were going to travel to a new country in a new hemisphere; I was entirely engrossed in getting out of Europe as soon as possible.

We knew we could not leave until June because I had to finish my book. There was a boat leaving Cherbourg on 6th June. There were several disadvantages about this boat. It meant travelling to Cherbourg, all the way across France, it was rushing things to make the sailing and, the most important fact, she was a German ship. After being bombed by German planes in Barcelona we did not care for the idea of sailing for nineteen days under the swastika.

There were advantages. The cost was absurdly little. We could get third-class accommodation for as little as £19 each. A German boat was sure to be clean. I spoke fairly fluent German and felt I could hold my own with a bunch of Nazis.

Francesca unexpectedly took a hand. She said her cousin was a British consul in Germany and could arrange to get good accommodation for us. She said if we would put off sailing until 1st July, the next boat to leave, she and João would come with us.

I was doubtful. To begin with Francesca was one of those people who seemed to take up a craze and then lose interest. We saw a fair amount of her and naturally most of our conversation was about Mexico. Before we thought of going to Mexico, Francesca had been interested in the idea of renting our hotel in Spain. We explained that we did not know if it was ours to rent, and we pointed out that conditions in Spain were not encouraging to tourists. Also we were convinced that Spain would support Germany in the event of war. Francesca, a Catholic, could not quite believe that the Christian Gentleman, Franco, could behave in such a dastardly manner, but several of our accounts of what went on in Spain during the war had shaken her. She decided that Mexico was a better bet.

The only choice for João was Mexico, or somewhere in Portugal, or out of Europe. It was tough to get work anywhere but there seemed to be a better chance in a country like Mexico. We told Francesca we did not know. We did not want to persuade her one way or the other. We told her that we would love to have her with us, because we had grown very fond of her, but that we could not possibly tell whether she would like Mexico, whether the climate would suit her, or whether the height would upset her. We had just begun to hear about the famous *altura*. She decided to take a chance and asked us to wait for the boat sailing 1st July.

I went for a long walk. Archie did not care. He slightly preferred to wait in order to have longer to get our papers, so it was up to me to decide. I wanted to oblige Francesca. She admitted that she would probably never get around to coming out by herself. But I wanted to leave France. I was tired of the sick feeling every morning waiting for the newspaper to come to see if the war had started. My instincts told me to cut and run for the June boat, even if it meant bad accommodation. Then I thought it would be unfair to Francesca and João not to wait until they could get their papers fixed up. It certainly would be a more comfortable arrangement to wait. Finally I decided. We would wait until the later boat, but no longer. We would sail for certain on the *Iberia*, on 1st July 1939.

Chapter 4
Goodbye to the Children

We had news from some of our refugee friends. Nikolaus, a German friend from Tossa, had arrived in Nice. He was homesick for Barcelona and was trying to arrange to get back. We thought he was crazy. The Marks were in London. Marianne and Ulrich, whom we had helped to escape, were scratching a living in Paris with no permanent papers and in constant fear of being picked up by the police. Captain Arjona, the officer who had come back at the risk of his life to rescue us and the children just before the Fascists entered our village, had been rescued thanks to the good work of the relief commission and was being shipped with his entire family to Mexico. We had asked our friends to do everything possible to get Arjona out of Argelès camp and to get him and his family away. Our friends responded nobly but we were not popular when it was discovered that the family consisted of eight children. However, all eight children eventually turned up on board the Sinai on the way to Mexico and we received postcards from each port from '*Arjona y su numerosa familia.*'

Our children were moved from their convent to a refugee camp near Besançon and we arranged to go to Paris that way in order to spend a few days with them. We hoped to be able to fix up something in Mexico for them. We had so enjoyed running the refugee colony in Spain we thought we might be able to do a similar job in Mexico. Francesca was thrilled with the idea and we were delighted to have her to help us. It was soon apparent that any arrangements would have to be done once we were in Mexico.

We heard from Rosita of the British Medical Unit in Spain that she was in England and wanted to come to Mexico whenever she could save up enough money. I shall always be grateful to Rosita for saving my typewriter when it, she and her house were thrown in a heap by a bomb. We told her that we would send her all the information we could once we were in Mexico.

Our ex-hotel-partner, Leon, was in England looking after Basque children. We wanted him to come with us. He could not decide. He thought that he would wait until he heard from us, once we were in Mexico.

It seemed that there was nothing more to be done from Europe. We could get our papers arranged by the Mexican consulate in Paris; we had booked accommodation on the *Iberia* through Francesca's cousin in Germany. We had raised enough money to pay our passages and to settle our deposit of £70, with a little over to keep us going for a month. There was nothing else to be done until we were in Mexico.

Francesca and João went to Paris while we started on our cross-country journey to Besançon. They left with innumerable pieces of luggage. It seemed amazing that two people could have so many possessions. Then we remembered that it was quite usual for people to have more than two suitcases, a rucksack and a typewriter. The only surprise about Francesca having mountains of luggage was that she could never resist giving all her possessions away if she thought anyone needed them.

Archie and I were thrilled to be going to see the children. We had become very attached to them in Spain and we knew that we stood to them as something stable in a very uncertain world. We hated to break the news that we were going so far away but we were determined to see if we could not get Leonor and her daughter to Mexico eventually. The other children all had their parents somewhere in France and we had heard that at last contact had been established with all the parents.

The village near Besançon where the children had their new camp was in the most peaceful rural setting with neat, tiled houses and well-filled barns. In the centre there was an enormous walled-in château, once a Royal hunting lodge, which had been burned down years before. Now the grounds and the walls were used to harbour Spanish refugees.

We found a room in one of the village inns. It was a beautiful room with oak beams and a glorious view over the countryside. The patron told us that they had few visitors except occasional crazy writers, who seemed to like the peaceful atmosphere. We asked him what the local people thought about the probability of war. He shrugged and said he never thought of it. It was bad enough to have refugees in the village. The villagers had heard such tales about the wildness of the refugees that most people were afraid to go out at night.

His wife was more sympathetic. We told her that we had come there to see our children and she confessed that she felt sorry for the refugees.

'The guards say some of the women are fierce,' she told us, 'but I don't blame them. They don't get enough soap, and everyone knows a woman wants plenty of soap.'

We were uncertain just how to go about seeing the children. Knowing a little about officialdom in France, we realized that we should have documents signed by the Préfet of Doubs at Besançon. That meant an extra journey and several days' delay. We thought we would try what we could do without the Préfet's blessing. We still had our

National Relief Commission cards.

We paused under the giant porch while a sentry fetched someone higher in command. It seemed that it was unheard of for anyone to want to go in. While he was away we strolled casually nearer and nearer the actual entrance, which was wide open. By the time he returned with the administrator, we were well inside the grounds.

The administrator was extremely French. He personally would have no objection to our going in; he himself was only too anxious to be pleasant, but we could understand how things were. With these new and terrible responsibilities he could take no risks. He regretted, very much he regretted, that he could not let us in without a permit from the Préfet. After all, he assured us, he only had our word that we had ever had anything to do with any children in Spain. We might have the oddest intentions . . .

While he was talking, I had ventured even further into the grounds. Several children were playing in the distance. I said to Archie, 'Try one of your whistles.'

Archie has the street boy accomplishment of whistling through his fingers. The result is shrill and carrying. I saw the children stop dead. The administrator took a step backwards. Then children began running towards us from all sides.

I had thought, after the things I had seen in the Spanish war and later in the French camps, that nothing could move me deeply any more. But the sight of these children tearing through the trees and rushing down the broad avenue screaming 'Hachi! Nensi!' at the tops of their lungs was too much for me. Before I could actually burst into tears in front of the French soldiers, I was clasped to an ample bosom and tears poured all over me from Leonor. The children closed in; the administrator was nearly knocked down; a French sentry, bewildered but feeling there was a riot on somewhere, was knocked off his feet. When I at last emerged from the frantic tangle, Archie was fighting his way free of the delirious children and was being almost strangled by Leonor. We moved off down the avenue in a solid mass. No one made any attempt to stop us.

Those children were still behaving like angels. They had had two years of uncertainty and worry: first chased out of their homes by Fascist soldiers; then bombed and starved in Barcelona; then some months in our colony, well fed and happy; then newly captured by Fascists; then escaping in a small truck to a frontier town where we all lived for a week in a theatre which was destroyed by bombs fifteen minutes after we had evacuated it; then escaping to France where they were separated from us, their only friends, and pushed around to various refugee colonies, not knowing where their parents were or even if they were still alive. And through it all they were the best behaved, best disciplined set of children one could hope to find. They adored Leonor and they had confidence in us, although we could do nothing for them once we had taken them out of Spain. There were seventy of them altogether, aged from fifteen years to three and a half. When we visited them in France, Justo, aged three and a half, was sick. We saw him in hospital, still as far and red-faced as ever, with his adoring brother by his side. Even the hysterical French did not seem to think that Justo was planning anything terrible, even if he was a Spanish refugee. They looked after him well in the hospital.

Leonor told us that conditions were not good. There was a shortage of soap and several of the women refugees were protesting. The French authorities were not used to independent Spanish women and were terrified. Here, right in their midst, were all the terrors of the Spanish red terror. The women even refused to work until they had more soap. So the gates were closed and the guards were doubled.

Although all the children's colonies and women's colonies were together in this new camp, Leonor managed to keep our colony intact. She secured a small building which just housed them and which they kept shining and polished even without much soap. The elder girls helped to organize some kind of home life and we were amazed to find the colony functioning very much as it had in Spain. Only the setting was different. Instead of a lovely labour-saving house, they had a shack; instead of four children to a big airy room with closets and running water, they had their beds pushed together behind some curtains; instead of a tree-covered hillside leading down to the beach and the Mediterranean, they had an enclosure with high walls and sentries. But they managed to be happy. They had enough to eat although the food was not good. They had room to play and most of all, they still had Leonor.

We stayed three days in the village and spent all our time with the children. We bought food and had feasts; we even managed to persuade the administrator to let us take Leonor out to supper. If all our arrangements had not been made to go to Mexico, both Archie and I would have been happily settled in the village running our colony again. But it would have been impossible. We would have been up against the French authorities at every turn; we would not have been paid and we had to earn our living. We hated leaving. The children were marvellous. They were very quiet and the little ones cried by the older ones just held on to us very tightly and made us promise to write. We told

Leonor that whenever the red-faced children were finally settled with their parents we would move heaven and earth to get her out to Mexico.

Archie was silent in the train taking us to Paris. At last he said, 'Thank God we haven't any children.'

Chapter 5
Old Man in the Closet

Paris was more tranquil than the south of France. The French seemed to think the war was bound to start with an invasion by Italy and naturally the south was more concerned. Most people felt certain that war was inevitable but there had been so many scares. Paris had been roused to a war fever just before Munich; the general opinion seemed to be that unless there was a change of government in England there would be plenty more appeasement. There were still places to give away. No one believed that the Chamberlain Government would get roused about Danzig, which was listed as the next step for Hitler. In the meantime the people of Paris went on with their usual lives. They had sandbags stored on the top storeys and they had practised evacuating children. There was nothing for them to do but to wait and see what the British decided next.

Thanks to Francesca, we stayed in the small apartment belonging to some friends of hers who were still in the south of France. It was in the Duncan house, owned by the brother of Isadora Duncan, and we had no idea what that meant. The apartment was charming, right up on the roofs like in a René Clair film. I was given the key by an odd-looking person dressed in a sack tied round the middle, with a sort of duster round her head like a nun's coif. The key fitted two doors, one on each side of a narrow passage. The main door led into another narrow passage with two more doors. One was at the end of the passage and obviously led into the main part of the apartment. The other appeared to be in the outside wall of the building and I thought it must be a closet. I opened the main door and saw the three rooms; then I tried the closet door. The key did not fit and I went back to the outside door and tried that key. That did not fit either and I was thinking that it did not matter anyway, we did not need a closet, when the door shot open and a little man dressed in a black suit suddenly appeared.

'*Que voulez-vous?*' he asked severely. I did not want a thing. I was almost hysterical with surprise. While I was trying to apologize for disturbing him, he bolted back into the dark interior and slammed the door. I heard it being double-locked loudly.

I went thoughtfully into my new kitchen and looked at the window. It was one of the typical French dormer windows built out of the sloping roof. I climbed onto the window sill and had a good look at the outside roof and wall. There was another window jutting out about where the old man's door was. He presumably lived in the space of the window.

When I went downstairs I asked the strangely-clad lady with the sacking garment just what an old man was doing in the wall of my apartment. She laughed.

'He's an old soldier,' she informed me as if that explained it all. I discovered later that there is a French law that old soldiers cannot be turned out of their homes. This very old soldier had once owned all the house. Gradually he was pushed upwards and outwards. He ended up in the closet in my apartment.

He caused us no trouble at all. He only ventured out when he was sure neither of us would chance along the passage. He seemed scared to death of me. We forgot about him and were only reminded from time to time when a thin cough sounded through the old walls or rustling sounds came from behind the closed door.

The Duncan House is in the Rue de Seine in the Latin Quarter. It is like the setting of all the *Trilbys* and *La Bohèmes* rolled into one. But it goes further than that. It had Raymond Duncan.

Archie survived the shock of the duster-coifed lady with the sack, but one day he came up the stairs in a state of excitement. It was always exciting coming up the stairs, because on each floor there were rooms set aside for various cults and curiosities. One might rub shoulders with Friends of Buddha or pass the time of day with yogi. But Archie cared for none of these things.

'There's an even stranger old woman down in the yard,' he said. 'She wears a sack and sandals and has long grey hair with a gold band round it. And you'll never guess what she's doing.'

'You'll never guess who it is,' I said. 'That isn't an old woman. That's Raymond Duncan, and I certainly couldn't guess what he might be doing.'

'She, he, it,' said Archie, 'it's tinkering with an old Ford. There's something almost spiritual about the whole scene.'

'You know, I sometimes think we are luck to have only an old soldier in our closet,' I said.

We spent our evenings at the Dôme Café to pick up our friends. The first night we were there we saw Miguel strolling through the crowds. The last time we had seen him was on a motorcycle in a pair of Archie's trousers, after he had escaped from Barcelona three days after the Fascists entered the town. His own clothes were in rags and he rode away up the coast to report to army headquarters, if he could locate them, dressed in Archie's corduroy pants. Miguel is over six feet and Archie is five foot eight.

Miguel strolling among the crowd did not look as if he had ever been reduced to Archie's pants. He wore a beautiful suit and looked at peace with the world. He told us that he hoped to get Concha, his wife, and their new baby out of Barcelona. She was going to try to slip over the Pyrenees and hoped to escape along the old smugglers' passes. Anything was better than staying in Barcelona.

'Miguel,' we had to ask. 'Where did you get that marvellous suit?'

He grinned. 'I lifted it off a non-intervention observer at the frontier.'

Our visits to the Dôme were exciting and heart-breaking. We met many of our old friends and we could do nothing for any of them. We wanted to persuade Leon's parents to come to Mexico, but they felt it was far away and for the moment they had to work in Paris. We felt all the time that war was bound to come, but at the same time we would not give anyone advice. It seemed ironical that the people who had the means to go to Mexico were hesitant and others, like Marianne and Ulrich, who were desperate to get away, had no papers.

'You might be able to do something for us when you get to Mexico,' said Ulrich. He had never forgotten how we had worked an apparent miracle in Barcelona when Marianne developed pleurisy. She was in a hospital there, the upper storeys of which had been destroyed by bombs and the only food she got was hard chickpeas. Thanks to various friends of ours he had got an ambulance to take her into France and we had managed to give her enough money to keep her going for a time. We had then smuggled Ulrich out of Argelès concentration camp to join her.

We promised to do everything possible for them, but we

were not hopeful. Mexico was letting in thousands of Spaniards and was careful about other nationalities. It seemed to be impossible to get into Mexico without papers. We were thrilled to be going to a new country but the thought of leaving our best friends in such hopeless circumstances was depressing. It seemed so unfair that these people, who had risked their lives and their security for their ideals, should suffer while we travelled smugly around with British passports. We went to the Mexican Legation feeling wretched and guilty.

We asked to see the Mexican Minister. We had learned that it usually pays to start at the top. The clerk looked surprised and did not think the Minister usually saw people but we persuaded him to take in our names. He came out again, his brown eyes positively melting. The Minister would see us immediately. The Minister could hardly wait. In fact, the Minister was thrilled.

We went into the Minister's sanctum. We were mystified but complacent. We seemed to have chosen the right country after all. I walked in first and put on my best smile. A little, dark man rushed at us. It was Archie he wanted.

'Hachi!' he cried.

'Gabriel!' cried Archie, for once shaken out of his Scottish calm.

They slapped each other's shoulders and cooed over each other for some time. Gabriel had met us in Barcelona where he was trying to collect material for newspaper articles. Archie had shown him the ropes occasionally and he thought Archie was wonderful. We had had him to stay for a weekend and he thought Tossa was wonderful. I cooked him *arroz catalan* and had remembered to put in hot peppers and he had thought I was wonderful. So everything in the Mexican Legation was wonderful.

Our reception in the Mexican Legation was exceptional because of our associations with Gabriel, but we gathered that they try to be as pleasant as possible even with perfect strangers. The contrast with the British Consulate in Paris was overwhelming. We had passed by the British Consulate to get our passports endorsed for Mexico and South American countries. The British Consulate in Paris has a reputation for being snooty, but when we went there they were simply ill-mannered. I went up to the desk where a languid young man was scaring the wits out of an old lady. She was terrified because she had filled up the wrong forms and the young man was treating her like a school teacher returning a bad pupil's lessons. I left the unpleasant scene and approached another young man who was staring into space.

'I want these passports endorsed, please,' I said.

The young man continued to stare. I must admit that any British consulate is apt to bring out the worst in me. The prevailing attitude that a British consulate is there primarily for its own affairs and that British subjects are a tiresome incident in the day's work always irritates me. I became extremely British, and County British at that (I haven't been brought up in the country for nothing).

'Would you please attend to these passports?' I asked, in the ringing tones of the British upper-classes. The young man did not quiver. I sighed. I approached even nearer and recalling my schooldays in Paris, I asked in French. The young man jumped as if he had been shot. *He* looked at me and said with extreme haughtiness in Oxford English: 'Passports stamped? Certainly.'

'Why,' I said with wide-eyed surprise. 'You do speak good English!'

The young man went scarlet. 'I am English,' he cried

with almost a show of animation.

'Oh, hard of hearing,' I said sympathetically.

He took the passports without another word. He loathed me. He asked me with hate in his voice to enumerate the countries in South America which I wanted put in the passports. I said all of them. No, I couldn't remember all their names. Didn't he know? Well, put as many as he could think of. Oh yes, and Cuba, of course. He mustn't forget Mexico because that was where I was really going. I probably would never get around to going to any of the other places but it costs the same to have them all put in the passport. He wrote furiously while the frightened old lady looked in with fascination. She began to take heart. After all, these were only clerks. I heard her say in her thin English voice, 'But I won't copy it out again. Just cross out those lines.'

Francesca came in just as the clerk was finishing with my passport. She seemed surprised to see the elegant young man actually working and more surprised at my lofty attitude. Afterwards she told me that the Consulate in Paris is well known for treating its nationals like something blown in by an ill wind.

'You know, Francesca,' I exclaimed. 'I'm not anti-British. I dislike the British upper-classes, and British officials abroad are impossible. But I really like the British people. Only I can't stand the way they put up with all this nonsense.'

'But after all, the Consul General is a very important person,' said Francesca, who had a tremendous respect for institutions.

'Why, you help pay his salary out of your taxes,' I said.

'I hadn't thought of that,' said Francesca.

Chapter 6
Once in Mexico

We left Paris on 2nd July 1939. We left a calm Paris, only slightly shaken by the series of shocks of the war of nerves. The Quartier was gay with noisy students; the cafés were crowed with the usual mixture of refugees, intellectuals and homosexuals. Tourists thronged the main boulevards; droves of schoolgirls packed the museums. There was racing at Longchamps and polo at St Cloud. The police as usual were arresting large numbers of foreigners who either had no papers or who had left their papers in their hotels. Paris was nearly normal.

Francesca and João were suffering from vaccinations. One of the many requirements for entering Mexico was a certificate to show that one had been vaccinated. We gathered from friendly officials at the Mexican consulate that it was a formality but that some sort of certificate was necessary. Neither Archie nor I have any objection to being vaccinated but we did not want to spoil our last visit to Paris. Archie took charge.

In a street where brothels alternated with doctors' establishments, Archie found a doctor. We went into an airless French waiting-room massed with stuffed birds and dead flowers. Presently the doctor received us. We walked into his consulting room, our healthy tan from the blasts of Saint-Raphael fairly shining. He was a little old man with a bushy beard. He eyed us over the beard in some surprise.

'Er, which one of you is ill?' he asked mildly.

We explained that we were in perfect health. Archie suggested that he give us a certificate of vaccination. We both had vaccination marks. Archie's dated from the war of 1914-1918, mine were at least twenty years old.

The doctor was willing to sign anything but he explained that the vaccination was out of date. Archie said that was quite unimportant. We simply wanted papers with signatures and stamps. Had the doctor a selection of stamps?

The doctor was amused. He wrote us out and signed two beautiful documents saying he had witnessed our marks. He suggested if we really were so interested in stamps that we go to the local police to get his signature certified. Archie was delighted with the idea and we paid ten francs and went to the police. They took in the situation with French seriousness and asked us to call again. We came back in an hour and hardly recognized the papers. They were stamped and restamped, and the chief of the police had a particularly pleasing signature. We put the papers carefully away with our passports and Mexican tourist cards.

Gabriel had suggested that we go into the country on tourist cards. He arranged our and Francesca's and João's without any trouble. He explained that Mexico was a strange country. It was difficult to do very much at this end, but 'once in Mexico'—'*una vez en Mexico*'—it was a refrain. Gabriel said it; the clerks said it; our friends said it; it seemed that anything could be arranged in Mexico. The tourist cards were valid for six months. And after that time a tourist was supposed to collect his deposit of £35 and depart. But it seemed that once in Mexico it was possible to have the cards extended for another six months. And after that well, *una vez en Mexico.*

We left Paris with three suitcases (we had borrowed an extra one from Francesca) a rucksack and my typewriter.

We also had with us Francesca in her black hat, João in Saint-Raphael suitings and twenty-seven pieces of luggage. Cherbourg seemed full of charming officials of the Hamburg-Amerika line. It was a shock to us to meet our first Nazis. We had met Nazi spies, people with Nazi-like behaviour, and quantities of Germans who were not Nazis. This was the first time we had met the real thing. Here they all were, living, breathing supporters of the Third Reich.

We appreciated the German propaganda sense. The officials were not only un-Nazi, they were positively un-German. They were courteous, helpful and even amusing. We shook ourselves and thought we should meet the real Nazis on board.

We saw the *Iberia* as she lay outside the harbour. There is something exciting about seeing a ship for the first time when one realizes that for nineteen or twenty days every moment will be spent on board. The *Iberia* looked minute. She was 11,000 tons. We had no eyes for our fellow-passengers as we crowded onto the tender to take us aboard. I did notice an untidy young man with Slavonic features because he kindly offered to carry one of the suitcases. There was also a pretty girl who talked to everyone in some incomprehensible tongue. She had travelled down with us in our compartment but I did not notice her among the crowd on the tender. We climbed aboard. An Aryan-looking young purser greeted us with clicked heels and correct bow. The German flag with the swastika fluttered overhead. An appallingly grim photograph of the Fuehrer glared down at us from the first-class saloon. We were on our way to Mexico but we were not yet out of Europe.

We were pleased with our accommodations. Francesca had so scared us with awful stories of third class accommodations that we were prepared to be delighted with almost anything. Her cousin had secured us two-berth cabins which were tiny but comfortable, the only drawback being that they were inside. Only four- and six-berth cabins had ports. We did not bother much about this, because through the bay all the ports were kept closed.

Francesca was a seasoned traveller. She gave one look at her tiny cabin and decided that she was sick. She sent me for the ship's doctor. He was a delightfully shy young man who was rather pleased to have something to do. He hurried to the prostrate Francesca and agreed that she would be better off in the hospital. Francesca had armed herself with a letter from her Paris specialist written in his own crabbed handwriting and in French. We took it for granted that the doctor could read French and the handwriting and he was too shy to say he had no idea what was in the letter. So Francesca removed to the hospital where she slept in queenly state in a large stateroom with real windows.

I was on the look-out for a Nazi. The purser was so blond he positively shone, but his manners were perfect. The doctor was just a charming boy and his hair was dark. Our cabin steward was Portuguese; our table steward was like a Raphael cherub with soft brown eyes and the deck steward was being particularly pleasant to some Spanish refugees.

The first few days until we reached Lisbon I was scurrying round looking for a Nazi. I even told the stewards that I was a red refugee. They were either amused and said tch suiting's with tolerant laughter or they came very close and asked in hoarse whispers, 'Do you know any new funny stories about Hitler?'

That was the sure way to popularity on that ship. Funny stories about Hitler took the place of dirty stories. A group of people sniggering in a corner were sure to be telling funny stories about Hitler. It was extraordinary. The blond purser came over to where I was reading Max Werner's *Military Strength of the Powers*. It was the Left Book Club edition from London and dealt in detail with the Red Army. He asked me if he might borrow it when I was through. I looked so surprised that he explained, 'Of course it is not allowed in Germany, but on the high seas it is different.'

It certainly was different on the high seas. Our quarters were in the bows of the ship and near the crew's quarters. The sailors had excellent quarters and several of them had radio sets. There was no restriction on programs and however ignorant the people of Germany may be kept, the sailors certainly knew what was going on in the world—or at least as much as people in other countries knew.

I became friendly with all the stewards. One of them explained that very few of the ship's personnel belonged to the Nazi party.

'We are mostly from Hamburg,' he said. 'There are few Nazis in Hamburg. But we have one or two in the ship. The first officer is a Nazi and we have our political commissar.'

This was greeted with roars of laughter. My steward friend explained, 'He is very sad. No one will speak to him.'

'Which is he?' I asked.

'He is the doctor's assistant in the hospital,' I was told.

That explained why the blond young man had been so upset when he found Francesca in the hospital. She had slept happily in the airy room and the poor assistant had come in without warning that the hospital was occupied. He not only found Francesca but also João, who had had a bright idea. He thought that if his mother was sick and in hospital she might need something in the night, so João, fully clothed, keeping his large feet carefully sticking out at the end of the bed, went to sleep in the other bed. It was an upsetting sight for any Nazi commissar. He had been most German and formal and forced João to retire to his own room. Francesca merely passed out on him in a convenient manner and when the doctor came he gave orders that she was to remain. But the assistant never reconciled himself to the disorganization of law and order.

The poor assistant had a dreary time. The ship's company were a gay bunch, and every night after supper everyone proceeded to get drunk on beer. Quantities of beer were rolled in barrels along the decks to the third-class bar. The crew popped up out of their quarters and swilled beer; the stewards sat round the table in our dining room and drank and drank; the second-class bar was crowded with first-class stewards and the bands; the first-class bar was full of the officers. The captain was a grey-haired, silly-looking old man with a glassy look in his eye. He was never to be seen without a glass of whiskey before him and a large, domineering lady by his side. She was the Most Important Passenger. She was also the mother of the Most Attractive Girl. The old captain seemed to be so drunk and the crew grew so wild towards nightfall, that I wondered who steered the ship. My steward told me that all sorts of things happened to that ship. She used to be on the South America run and once, instead of making Curaçao harbour, she piled up on the island of the same name. It appeared that almost anything might happen on the *Iberia*. But the steward told me that given good officers she was a handy ship. She was all set to be converted into a mine-layer the moment war was declared.

The ship's personnel may have been anti-Nazi but there was no doubt about its attitude with regard to a war. My steward was genuinely shocked by the behaviour of Britain and France. Everyone I spoke to took it for granted that Hitler would take over Danzig at any moment. If Britain and France objected, that was just too bad. Everyone liked anti-Hitler stories but no one denied that Hitler was a great man. He had accomplished everything he set out to do; he had won back Germany's self-respect. Everyone was unanimous in approving the *Anschluss* in Austria and the annexation of Czechoslovakia; Danzig obviously was in the same category.

I asked about Spain. Everyone seemed reluctant to discuss Spain. At last someone said, 'Well, that was business.' That seemed to sum up their attitude over Spain. They were ashamed and they were extra pleasant to the Spanish refugees. They gave them special attention at meals and the deck steward worked overtime shifting chairs for sea-sick Spaniards. I was questioned closely about the air-raids and bombardments. I said frankly that I had not liked the idea of travelling on a German ship because my only experience with the Nazis had been the raids in the Spanish war. Everyone asked me eagerly, 'Were they really so bad? Did they use those new high explosive bombs?'

I was assured that anything used in Spain was now out of date. The latest type of airplane was something amazing. The German army was superb. Even the cook's boys knew that when the war came the British and French were going to get a big surprise. I smiled and said that fighting Britain and France would not be the same as fighting Spain. Britain and France would not be strangled for munitions and arms. There would be no non-intervention to help the Germans.

Archie and I realized more than ever that the German

people were a long way from dissatisfaction. They might be short of certain food essentials and the shadow of the Gestapo might loom over their homes, but Germany was becoming greater every day. Anyone who had seen the hopeless misery of the Germans in 1929 and 1930, the only time I have visited Germany, would realize just what Hitler's successes meant to those people. Germans do not mind starving for a 'greater' Germany. Men on the *Iberia* admitted that their families were short of butter, but they were proud to think that they were sacrificing something to aid the rise of the German Empire. Men like Chamberlain and Léon Blum killed any chance of internal uprising by continually allowing Hitler to succeed as surely as the City of London provided the money for the new weapons the stewards talked about so glibly.

Everyone was prepared for war at any moment, but there was no nervousness. The sailors seemed to think that Britain might be foolish enough to protest when Hitler went into Danzig; the officers on the whole thought that it would not provoke a war. No one doubted that war was coming shortly. The *Iberia* was even prepared to turn back. Once we were past the Azores and well into the Atlantic, one of the officers told me that what ever happened we would get to Havana. This far across it would be safe to proceed.

We were thankful. Hitler actually took Danzig when we were near Havana, which cut short our stay there as the ship had orders to hurry to Vera Cruz. Just beyond the Azores the *Iberia* suddenly swung right off her course. We saw two large warships to port. They seemed stationary and the *Iberia* made a detour to avoid them. Several sailors were discussing the warships and they seemed to come to the conclusion that they were Italian.

'The very latest type,' one told me enthusiastically. 'You see the small airplane in the stern.'
Then an officer hurried up with glasses.
'French,' he said disgustedly.
'Entirely old-fashioned and out of date,' said the sailor.
I had a great time on board. I am just the type that Nazis like: blond, healthy and athletic. I speak good enough German for Germans to think I come from some obscure German state. They thought that my insistence that I was a red refugee was a really funny joke. Germans have a heavy sense of humour. The passengers were a dull crowd. First class was dominated by the mother of the Most Attractive Girl, which meant that the officers had no chance at all; second class was chiefly full of overblown Cubans, the officers ranked as something below the honorary-Aryan Italians; third class was out of the question for the officers except for me and I was obviously in a class by myself.
I admit I encouraged the officers. I had the run of the ship which meant that Archie and our friends could use first or second class for dancing in the evenings. I was also getting some fine first-hand information about Germany and conditions under the Nazi regime. I was extremely strict and moral. When they made particularly violent passes at me I said that nothing would induce me to commit *Rassenschande*, or shaming of the race, which is what happens in Germany if an Aryan has an affair with a Jew. They laughed and said they refuse to believe I was Jewish.
'Oh no,' I said, 'it isn't that. You see, for us reds to have affairs with Nazis would be too shaming for words. Far worse than what you call *Rassenschande*, in fact.'
I was not so popular with the officers after that.

Chapter 7
Street-Car Frolic

It was a perfect voyage. The sea was smooth, like watered silk, except for days when it glittered like a cut diamond. A soft breeze tempered the sun and Archie and I spent all day on the forward hatches. First and second classes shared a magnificent swimming pool in the stern, but third class had a canvas pool rigged up on deck which we used all day long. The Spaniards huddled under tarpaulins to keep out of the hated sunshine, so we had the deck practically to ourselves except for occasional visits from Francesca and João and the Slavonic-looking young man who had helped me to carry one of my bags on the tender.

He turned out to be a Russian with a complicated name, so we called him Vladivostok for short. He was a most superior young man. His people were Russian refugees and he was a very White Russian, which perhaps accounted for his peculiarities. He did not speak much but when he did it was to relate how he was supreme at some particular branch of athletics or history or physics. He had a disdain for all branches of literature. Between Cherbourg and Lisbon he dwelled on his superiority in swimming and diving; after the pool was fixed up he looked on with a superior smile while I disported myself in the small tank and he decided that the pool was too small for his talents. He was always profoundly occupied with some learned tome and he indicated that he required the deepest solitude in order to study. Unfortunately it was too easy to find obscure corners on a ship, which meant that he could study all day and no one would ever know. So he chose the other extreme and sat as near to us as possible, acquiring a beautiful tan, if nothing else.

We had occasional discussions. He considered himself a refugee and he could not see that there was the world of difference between him and the Spanish refugees. He complained that the Spaniards were making the same error as the Russian refugees. They could not consider settling permanently in any country because they always hoped that some day the old régime would come back. Vladivostok considered this a mistake. He was far-sighted enough to realize that the old regime in Russian was gone for ever and that people like himself who did not care for the new regime had to make their lives elsewhere. He could not see that this had nothing to do with the Spanish refugees. He could not see that the Spaniards were not fleeing from a new régime but from the re-imposition of the old one in a different form. The Spaniards had to look forward to the day when the Franco administration, with its reinstating of the power of the Church and the rich landowners, would crash and they could return to carry on progress where they had been interrupted.

Vladivostok was kind to us. He played draughts with Archie, who beat him easily, and decided that we knew no better because we did not understand the values of class distinctions. He told us that he was poor (and certainly his clothes were dirty) but that he never forgot that his family was noble. He was going to Mexico to spend his holidays from his work in Paris with two beautiful, well-born English girls. We gathered that the English girls came from the cream of British aristocracy. It seemed almost a shame that poor Vladivostok had to waste twenty days on the high seas with such riff-raff as we in the third class.

As we neared Havana the weather became gloriously

hot. Our cabins were impossible at night, so we moved up on deck. We were told ghastly stories of people sleeping on deck and waking up in the morning with their limbs wracked and twisted by rheumatism; of other people who caught a malignant fever. The only risk seemed to be a bite by a flying fish. We decided that we would try it out.

Archie found a wonderful bed. He climbed up into a hammock made by the sag of a tarpaulin that covered two cars. Francesca crept into a lifeboat; I preferred the steamer chairs. Francesca was ignominiously ejected by the first officer, who happened to be looking from the bridge, so she managed to curl up her long legs in a steamer chair.

I had two attentive young men who insisted on putting their steamer chairs on each side of mine. One was a Spanish anarchist who had been in the secret police in Barcelona and the other was a naïve young man whose father was Mexican but who had been born and educated in England. He was not sure if it were absolutely correct for all of us to sleep up on deck in such a casual manner. He said to me rather nervously, 'You know, this is the first time I have ever slept next to a married lady.'

I was disappointed about the flying fish. I had read about flying fish and I was convinced that they were pink. I had visions of thousands of red mullet with silver wings fluttering above the waves. The real flying fish were sea-coloured and almost invisible as they skimmed the surface of the blue-green water. Otherwise the Hamburg-Amerika did us proud. We saw the dark funnel-shaped cloud of a cyclone travel rapidly away in the distance. When we approached sudden tropical rainstorms the captain ordered the ship off her course to avoid them.

I was sorry to reach Havana, but Archie, Francesca and Joao were looking forward to twenty-four hours on shore. Cuba is another country which is scared of refugees. In order to land at Havana one has to put up a bond of 500 dollars each. The ship will then give a pass. Between us we had about 500 dollars. We thought that we might manage to wangle something. Francesca and I went up to see the purser. The little blond purser was elsewhere, probably reading my Left Books. Francesca swept into the office. The other purser was sorry, he could do nothing without a bond of 500 dollars for each of us. Francesca became inches taller (she stands about six feet in her stockings) and looked down at the purser.

'How absurd,' she said. 'You know perfectly well you have my pearls in the safe. They are worth more than enough to cover us all.'

The purser was wilting when the blond purser came up. He settled it all immediately. Our passports and the 500 dollars would be enough for all of us. Francesca insisted on the pearls and offered her watch with devastating scorn. We were the only people on the ship who got passes without putting up the full bond.

We were fascinated to see the change in the first- and second-class passengers when we got to the tropics. They all burgeoned forth into tropical suits. Going-ashore clothes for Havana were something. One enormously fat Cuban was striding about the deck in a red linen sun suit with the price label stuck on the back of his pants. Mr Watkinson-Upwood managed to make even that look normal.

Mr Watkinson-Upwood was English. He was so English one could not even call him British. He travelled second-class, but he preferred our company, so he spent a good deal of his time on our deck. He asked us if he might accompany us ashore at Havana.

Mr Watkinson-Upwood appeared to go ashore in a brand new shantung suit for the tropics that was very much creased from packing; he wore a brand new Panama which had been rolled up in his baggage so that the brim was fluted. The black hatband still had the basting stitches in it. He had a pair of green sunglasses. And over his shantung arm, he carried a beautifully rolled black umbrella.

'I have been advised that sudden showers are frequent at this time of the year,' said Mr Watkinson-Upwood.

We proceeded along the main street of Havana much to the amusement of the inhabitants. Francesca strode along ahead, as usual beautifully dressed but looking enormously tall; Joao strolled along looking very French Riviera; Archie always looks neat, but he was dwarfed by Francesca; Vladivostok had tacked on to our party and wore a torn pair of linen trousers and a filthy crew-neck sweater that had once been pale blue; my sunburn and blond hair attracted much attention, and behind us, looking for a place to change money, walked Mr Watkinson-Upwood complete with umbrella.

The party began to get fretful. I had an idea. We went for a ride in a street-car.

Havana street-cars are like no other street-cars on earth. They are small and friendly, and the driver and the conductor become almost intimate by the end of a trip. The street-cars do not amble along streets. They dash madly out into the countryside where, by accident or design, the tracks are laid so as to give a switchback sensation. The little cars plunge and rear in the craziest way as they tear past old ladies rocking peacefully on their verandas, on and on for miles past gimcrack villas and half-finished gardens, until at last they reach a row of trees and the sea. Here is the beach.

The beach cannot be seen for the large Cuban ladies strolling over it. Cuban figures certainly are surprising. Archie and Joao began to enjoy themselves. Vladivostok seemed above earthly pleasures and Mr Watkinson-Upwood was upset because the banks were all closed.

I found the Cubans amazingly friendly. There is no visible colour-bar and there is a strong flavour of the childlike pleasure that seems to be found among coloured people. The policemen, in their starched, shiny blue jackets, radiate good-humour. I mentioned the policemen to a woman in first class who knew Cuba well. She assured me that they were as pleasant as they appeared.

'Sometimes if I was coming home from a party I would get a policeman to escort me. So charming, you know, always walked behind me and never once attempted any liberties.'

'What a shame,' I murmured without thinking.

We left Havana and started on our last stretch to Vera Cruz and Mexico. We were sailing through the Gulf of Mexico and in three days the voyage would be over. The ship had received orders to cut short her stay in Havana because Hitler had taken over Danzig. She would make a quick turn round in Vera Cruz instead of going up to Tampico in order to get home in readiness to be a minelayer.

I was longing to get Mexico but I hated to leave the ship. I always feel like that about ships. I don't have any particular craving to get on them, but I hate to get off them. Archie was longing to get ashore. He hated the German food, which was good and ample but thoroughly German, and he felt it was time to get to this Mexico.

Before reaching Havana we had threaded our way through the Bahamas. Low-lying, scrubby little islands appeared from time to time within a stone's throw of the ship. (One of Archie's throws, not mine. I never could throw stones.) I was on the bridge with the first (and Nazi) officer and he showed me our course

'The British make us pay through the nose to pass through here,' he said, indicating the narrow waterways between the islands.

'The British?' I said. 'Oh, do the British own the Bahamas?'

Now those were pre-Windsor days, and my laps was perhaps more pardonable than it would be today. But not as the first officer saw it. He never spoke to me again. I might look Aryan, I might speak good German, but a woman who did not know what her own country owned was out.

We shave Miami and the Florida keys and then sailed south to Havan. From there we sailed west, rounded the Yucatan peninsula, crossed the bay of Campeche, and arrived at Vera Cruz.

The first sight of Vera Cruz was a line of greyish mist on the horizon with the snow peak of Mount Orizaba in the background. Mexico was living up to its reputation. The second sight was the pier. Originally built of wood, it had so rotted and collapsed that only a few iron strips held it together. It seemed impossible that anyone could walk across it, let alone convey luggage. However, the local inhabitants seemed happy enough. They balanced on the cracked cross-pieces waiting for the ship to dock.

Coming from Europe and suddenly seeing a crowd of Mexicans is breath-taking. I felt like an English elderly friend of mine who told me that she was horror-stricken when she arrived at Vera Cruz ten years ago. She peered down at the dock and gave a shriek.

'My God, they are all black!'

I did not shriek that everyone was black. All I could see was a greater variety of hats than I had imagined possible.

Large sombreros predominated, but no two seemed to be alike. There was every stage of dilapidated straw, and then some cunning little numbers in chipped felt. These looked like aged fedoras with the brims removed and then the crown clipped into patterns.

Underneath this variety there seemed to be one face, squat-nosed, rheumy-eyed, thick-lipped. Vera Cruz waterfront workers are not beautiful. Their colour was certainly dark, but I was getting rather self-conscious about colour. I was browner than I had ever been in my life from lying all day in the tropical sun across the Gulf. If there was any colour-bar in Mexico, that went for me too.

There were endless formalities. The Mexican authorities came on board and sat behind long tables. Mario, the Mexican boy educated in England, was an angel of helpfulness. He could have got off the ship immediately, but he chose to stick around in case we needed help. We thought it was sweet of him, but we could not see why we might need help. We did not know the waterfront union.

Archie was delighted because the Mexican health authorities were charmed with our vaccination certificate. They looked at the still store marks on Francisca and Joao and were doubtful, but they decided to let it go. Mario had been vaccinated three months previously and had his certificate, but they pounced on him. They were only counting vaccinations ten days old that day. So Mario was led protestingly to the medical authorities to be revaccinated.

Our crowning triumph was when we saw the man about our bond for 175 dollars. We had the money all ready. He was about to take it and then he said: 'Why do you put up all this money? If you go to my colleague over there you can get another arrangement which will not need so much money."

We found that we could either hand 175 dollars each to a representative of a Mexican bank and receive the entire sum when we left the country at the end of our stay, or, if we preferred, we could hand over 33 dollars each and forfeit 7 dollars on the return of the money. The idea of having an unexpected 140 dollars each delighted us. 'Una vez en Mexico—' we said to ourselves.

Of course, we found later, a year later in fact, that we need not have deposited any money at all. A bonding company will take care of it all for a matter of five dollars.

Chapter 8
Typical Tropical Trips

Archie and I liked Vera Cruz. We liked it so much that we decided to spend an extra day there. We found out later that this is very unusual. Francesca and João ran truer to form.

Our introduction to the port was not auspicious. We nearly broke our necks getting from the ship to the customs shed, but we chose a good moment when the rickety pier was empty so we could pick our way from plank to plank. After our inspection by the Mexican authorities we decided that it was late and that we were hungry. Technically, we were no longer passengers on the ship, but we went aboard again and down to the third class to see if we could rustle up any food. Our stewards greeted us like long-lost brothers and immediately opened up the bar. The deck steward had been given a jar of caviar by a friend in the first class, there was the usual array of sausages, and we had quite a party. Thus fortified, we braved the broken pier again.

The customs were no trouble at all. The officials were somewhat stunned by the array of Francesca's luggage, but they were tired after a hard morning's work and they did not search thoroughly. However, one of them found our *boules*.

When we wrote to thank some friends for their detailed account of Mexico, we had politely asked if there was any little thing we might bring over from Europe. The deal friends asked for a set of Provençal *boules*. A set consists of eight steel balls the size of baseballs, each weighing about two pounds. We are kind to our friends, so we brought the set of *boules*. The customs man found one. He weighed it cautiously in his hand and eyed me suspiciously. It was the nearest thing to a bomb he had ever seen.

I explained it was a game. Other customs men gathered round. The first customs man produced yet another bomb-like object; I hastily told him that there were eight in all. And a little wooden one.

They wanted to see the game. Archie and I gravely rolled the *boules* around the concrete floor of the customs shed. We explained the rules. Soon our difficulty was to stop the customs men playing. We left in a flurry of compliments and goodwill.

We plunged immediately into the full blast of dockside syndicalism. Now Archie and I approve strongly of unions and syndicates. We liked running an hotel in Spain because the hotel employees' union was one of the strongest in Spain. We were not at all the sort of people to grapple with the porters' union in Vera Cruz.

We found out afterwards that unions in Mexico have their peculiarities. Some of them have run away from the original idea of a union and have become simply rackets. Vera Cruz water-front boys run a racket. They swoop down on baggage and charge exorbitant rates to carry them across the street. There are non-union men hanging around offering their services for about an eighth of the price, but we did not consider employing scab labour. We paid grimly. Francesca the grimmest of all because she had twenty-seven pieces of baggage, and anyway, she did not know what scab labour was.

We got to an hotel that looked as if it might manage to stand up throughout the night. Most of the other buildings did not. We were given a large double room for four pesos, about eighty cents in those days. It had a partition with a bath-tub and a shower and an electric fan.

The electric fan was a gladdening sight. It seemed to show that we were really in the tropics. We kept turning it on because that is the correct thing to do in the tropics, but then one or the other of us would switch it off absent-mindedly because of the draught. It just seemed that the Johnstones like heat.

Veracruzanos may be lacking in the good looks immortalized by Eisenstein in Thunder Over Mexico, but they are gay. The streets were filled with white-clad Indians with brown faces and splashes of white teeth. Archie and I were entranced listening to the soft, lilting Spanish, reminiscent of the lisping tones of Andalucía, when Mario, the Mexican-English boy, came up and joined us. He had nobly stood by while we went through the customs. He was taking the overnight train up to Mexico City. We decided to go up by day in order to see the views, and also we wanted to see more of Vera Cruz.

As we sat and sipped our drinks, we saw Vladivostok stroll by accompanied by two staggeringly beautiful girls. They wore embroidered Mexican shirts, full embroidered trousers, and colossal sombreros, dwarfing the everyday mushroom straws around them.

'Look, Archie!' I exclaimed. 'There are the very aristocratic young English ladies.'

We gazed over in admiration. Suddenly the tallest of the girls rushed over.

'Hello, Nancy,' she cried. 'What on earth are you doing here?'

She was an old school friend from Paris. Vladivostok's jaw dropped. To think he had crossed the Atlantic with someone who might even have been a drop of the skimmed milk of the British aristocracy and he had not known it!

We were still drinking when Mr Watkinson-Upwood was driven by in a large automobile.

Mr Watkinson-Upwood had informed us that he was visiting friends in Mexico City, American friends. We gathered that they were very important people who only moved in the best of circles. They had made their money mining. The head of the family came to Vera Cruz to meet Mr Watkinson-Upwood in his automobile.

They drove slowly across the top of the square. Mr Watkinson-Upwood sat bolt upright, still wearing his shantung suit, still wearing his frill-brimmed Panama, his hands crossed meekly over the handle of his umbrella. His host drove the car himself, leaning back behind the steering-wheel with easy nonchalance, a broad-brimmed hat pulled over one eye, an enormous cigar at an acute angle from thin lips above a jutting chin. America was taking England for a ride.

We told Mario that we would come to the station to see him off. We were just starting off when Joao appeared to say that Francesca could not stand Vera Cruz for another moment and wished to leave on the night train.

Then things moved in all directions. I rushed off to the station to try to get last-minute sleeping berths; Archie dashed madly to the hotel to help with the baggage. Joao helped Francesca repack her suitcase. I saw Mario at the station and he immediately left me in charge of his luggage while he took a cab back to the hotel to fetch them. I though it was strange to have to leave anyone guarding baggage, but I later learned better.

There were shouts and whistles from the train, which seemed about to leave, but I could do nothing but wait. At last a cavalcade arrived.

Francesca was at the head, looking utterly wild, carrying various undergarments which she had not been able to pack; Joao staggered behind with some of the luggage; Mario and two porters carried the rest. Archie was not there. He had already been to the station once and was by this time back at the hotel to collect all the things left behind. The train was about to depart.

They made it. Francesca snatched the tickets from me and swept into the train as it gathered breath to leave. João leaped in further down. Mario was involved in a violent fight between his porters who were outside the racket (Francesca had had enough of organized labour) and some of the inside men. The train started to slide out of the station. Mario suddenly leaped into the battle and began to bang everyone's heads together. Mario might be naïve but he could use his fists. He was the size of any two of the combatants. The battle broke up in disorder. Mario caught up the remaining baggage and just made the train as it gathered speed. Archie arrived as the train disappeared from view. He carried a bottle of eau-de-cologne, a cake of soap and a night-dress.

* * * * x

We had had all the warnings about insect life in the tropics. Beds would have bugs; some of the spiders were not poisonous; scorpions hid in shoes. The only things we saw in Vera Cruz were giant roaches in the bathroom but as they fled down the drain of the shower whenever the light was turned on, we did not care.

Vera Cruz seemed swell to us. We went out to the beach during the day but bathing was impossible because the Gulf stream is too hot. One suffocates trying to swim. So we spent most of our time sucking coconut milk through straws and watching the people. Coconut milk seemed to have an odd effect on Archie who sat in the sunshine drivelling to himself. 'Typical tropical trips—topical trips to the tropical tropics—triple traffic in topical trips to the typical tropics—'

Vera Cruz has a gay *paseo*. The girls march around arm in arm in one direction and the young men walk the opposite way, calling out remarks to all the pretty girls. A band plays up above on a terrace but it is almost drowned by the shrill voices of the Veracruzanos. There was an atmosphere of light-heartedness that reminded us of Spain. We smiled at the stories we had heard about the dourness of the Indians.

Reading and the movies have taken a lot of the zest out of travelling. We seemed to take it for granted that coconuts grew on the palm trees along the shore and that the milk was delicious sucked through straws. The sight of men selling stage parrots of red and green, or blue and yellow, was picturesque but not surprising. The carried the parrots perched on long sticks and apparently quite tame. Banana trees heavy with fruit and piles of fresh pineapples at the street corners were to be expected in the tropics. Both Archie and I appreciated everything but we did not exclaim in wonder.

From my earliest youth I have wanted to taste a fresh mango. Friends and relations in the far-flung British Empire have raved about mangos. I had a chance in Havana but I got in a panic. After thinking about fresh mangos for all these years, what a tragedy if I dislike them! I could not bear to risk smashing an illusion. I decided to forgo a mango in Vera Cruz. Some day, when surrounded by mangos, I would venture to put the illusion to the test.

Everyone has read or seen pictures of the deep jungle. Everyone knows how a cunning rope-like vine is always there for the hero to swing himself out of reach of the rhinoceros, or over a cliff, or up the cannibals' stockade. On our trip from Vera Cruz to Orizaba on the way to Mexico City we actually saw these ropes hanging from every tree, cliff and precipice. We found out that not only are they perfectly real, but they are the roots of plants trying to reach water.

The amazing journey to Orizaba is hard to describe. I had read several accounts of it before I actually found myself in a train climbing the four thousand feet in four hours, and I was not in the least prepared for the extraordinary trip. Archie and I were entranced by every foot of the way.

We started through the Tierra Caliente, or hot country, which is between sea-level and 3,000 feet, and the vegetation seemed the most bizarre and luxurious in the world. Every scene seemed especially arranged for the train passengers. One had the impression that once the train had passed everything flicked back to normal. The tree with leaves the size of elephants' ears, the bush completely covered with wide white flowers, the crimson and gold birds posed among deep-blue blossoms, the rank growing palms, the beautifully shaped Jacaranda tree with its grey-blue branches vanishing in clouds of smoky purple, must have all been set up a few hours before. The bronze woman with the white flowing skirt and deep blue rebozo shawl over her black hair, the little boy with no pants riding a pantomime donkey, the aged Indian in his stiffly starched blouse and enormous hat, they must have run laughing to change back into their everyday drabness the moment the train was past.

But when we reached the Temperate Zone, up another thousand feet, there was no question of anything having been staged. It seemed as if the train must hurry before bushes sprouted in the tracks or it became entangled in a vine. We cut through the sheer mountainside, crossing ravines on bridges that seemed to be held up by the dense growth. Below us we could see coffee plantations, fields of sugar cane and here and there the bright green of rice fields. At every station women thronged the train selling eatables, all with names and appearances unintelligible to us, or carrying clusters of orchids as carelessly as if they were a bunch of daisies. Banana stems, split open and packed with gardenias, were sold for 1 cent. The train climbed through banana groves, the trees heavy with fruit, always curving round and round the switchback. The women at the station ran straight up the mountainside and were waiting at the next station with their strange assortment of eatables, their orchids, and their gardenias.

We fell in love with Fortin, a tiny village on the edge of the jungle. We decided that if we could not make a living in the more civilized parts of Mexico, we would retire to Fortin and live in a palm-leaf hut overgrown with orchids. Both Archie and I like a hot-house atmosphere and we have a passion for growing things. The only drawback to Fortin seemed to be how to control the growth. It would be alarming to find a papaya tree sprouting up through one's bed in the morning.

Once past Orizaba we teetered for a while on the ridge of the mountains and then we crossed to the plain beyond them. We were still rising, but now we were approaching the Tierra Fria, or cold country. We put on overcoats and watched the endless procession of maguey plants as we raced along at eight thousand feet above sea-level. We mounted still higher before we dropped down into the Valley of Mexico, guarded by the two volcanoes, Popcatepetl and Ixtaccíhuatl. We caught a bare glimpse of them, patches of snow showing dimly in the evening haze. Then we began to pass more little adobe houses, an abandoned or ruined one for every three finished ones. Giant magueys raised spiky fences round the mud-coloured huts; with the draining of the lakes that used to floor it,. The trained pulled slowly into a modern station. We collected our few belongings and stepped out on to the platform. We almost stepped on Richard Rees.

'Hello,' said Richard amiable. 'This is very luck indeed. I am just leaving for New York.'

Chapter 9
Everybody Gets Everything

Richard Rees looked very sick.

'And how did you get here?' we asked. 'You were almost the only one of our friends who decided *not* to come to Mexico.'

Richard explained he had come over to see about conditions for Spanish refugees. He had come via New York, which cut days off his journey, and beat us easily.

'Must you rush back?' we asked. 'Can't you stay over a couple of days? There is so much we want to know about the refugees.'

Richard shuddered. 'Dysentery,' he said.

'Do most people get dysentery?' we asked.

'Everyone does,' said Richard gloomily.

Richard's train was due, so we went to see him off. He explained that conditions for the refugees were not too good but that everyone hoped things would improve. He was going back to England to make his report to the London committee. He would also report that we had arrived in Mexico and were ready to do any work that was necessary.

Richard was nearly left behind to the altitude and dysentery. He stood on the little wooden footstool outside the steps to the train and waved goodbye as the train pulled out. We laughed so much we could not tell him what was happening, but he realized something was wrong and hastily leaped into the train.

'Don't try to run or anything,' he shouted as the train gathered speed.

'Why not run?' I asked Archie.

'The altitude,' said Archie. 'It seems that we are a mile and a half above sea level.'

I looked up and saw someone walking away with our luggage. I sprinted down the long platform and found it was Joao, who had come to meet us. He and Francesca had found a small hotel which was cheap and free from bed bugs.

'They say you shouldn't run hear,' he said doubtfully.

'They say a lot of things,' I said.

That evening we ran into my ex-schoolmate, her sister, Vladivostok, a German, and a Frenchman in the Cucaracha bar. We had a gay evening and I noted the Cucaracha bar as a place to remember. Unfortunately I was unable to locate it again for month. It became a sort of game, and I refused to ask anyone to take me there. When I did find it I could not imagine what the difficulty had been.

We stayed two days in Mexico City. There did not seem to be anything special about it. There were a number of American tourists roaming the streets, a large number of vendors of an assortment of sticky candies which most Mexicans seemed to be chewing as they walked along, some smart young men exactly like smart young men in any city, some suave businessmen just like suave businessmen anywhere. The chief difference of Mexico City from any European capital is that there is an appearance of new-richness about the buildings and the streets are jammed with beautiful cars.

We learned that he first thing a Mexican does when he makes any money is to buy a car. Sometimes he will own two or three cars and live in a tenement. Practically never does he learn to drive a car well. He learns to manoeuvre it around Mexico City and to play a little phrase on the horn about what should be done to other people's mothers.

The Rioja Hotel is a small Mexican hotel mostly used by miners in town to raise money or to sell stones, and by the foremen of sugar mills or coffee plantations. The proprietors are Spanish and they are sympathetic to refugees. When they heard that we were in effect refugees they cut down their prices and gave us a good room with running water for 40 cents for both of us.

We decided to go down to Cuernavaca with some friends for the weekend. Francesca, who was in a panic that we might think she was 'tacking on' to us, decided to go on to Taxco. She had spent the days we were in Vera Cruz at all the tourist agencies and had duly registered at the British Consulate. We decided we could dispense with that ceremony. The changes were that the consulate knew all about us. We had helped in our small way to get one Consul-General in Barcelona removed. It seemed too much to expect that the Consulate in Mexico would welcome us.

The drive to Cuernavaca was a good forty cents' worth. The car climbed up from Mexico City about another thousand feet, letting us have a view over the whole valley of Mexico hemmed in by distant mountains. The two volcanoes stood out clearly in the sunlight, Ixtaccíhuatl, the Sleeping Woman, uncannily like a giant goddess sprawling on her back with her white hair flowing. Popocatepetl was more elegant, the conventional volcano with symmetrical sides and snow-covered tip. Both of them looked two-dimensional, flat against the sky. I expected to see the dark shadow of the teacher's pointer as he explained the lantern show.

Little rounded hills with hollows in their summits spring up all round the valley of Mexico, showing clearly the great upheavals and convulsions that made the great mountains.

It is easy to imagine the boiling, bubbling mess that musts have been before the present contours emerged. The Mexican landscape relies for its beauty on the play of light on these contours. That is why it continually changes. The first day we looked across the Mexican plain the light was shining flatly on the hills, making them stand out clearly as in a lithograph.

We reached to top of a range mountains and the road ran for a time past the easy undulation of scrub grass and pine trees. A crazy railroad track spun around the road, crossing and recrossing until it was impossible to guess if it was coming or going. Our driver slowed carefully at each crossing but there was no sign of any train. Cuernavaca had a station. The train took six hours to get to Mexico City, fifty miles away.

There seemed to be no sign of life in the mountains. The scrub grass is useless for fodder but it is used to thatch the mud huts. We came upon a village set close to the road. The houses were made of adobe or mud, with corrugated iron roofs instead of grass. It was without exception the most desolate village I have ever seen. The inhabitants stood in their doorways staring into space through narrow slits between the sombreros pulled down to their eyebrows and the sarapes pulled up to their eyes. There was a soft drizzle falling which was swept aside every now and then by a blast of wind. We grabbed our coats and pulled them round our necks. The car began to coast down hill. We turned two snake-like turns and began to drop from four thousand feet to Cuernavaca.

The road loops through wooded hills. The trees hide the view until a sudden turn floods one with the brilliance of the plain of Morelos.

Cuernavaca lies among trees on a platform just below

the big mountains. Below the platform, or terrace, the plain stretches away for thirty miles, always dropping a little, until it reaches a big range of mountains that stretch from east to west like a wall. Beyond those mountains lies Taxco in the state of Guerrero which reaches the Pacific coast. The Morelos plain is a patchwork of colours, varying according to the season, rainy or dry. We saw it first towards the end of the rainy season, when every scrap of earth sends up green shoots. Stretches of emerald, the sugar cane fields, were outlined with the yellow-green of banana trees or the blue-green of magueys. Brilliant patches of bougainvillea caught the setting sun; the mountains turned mauve against the turquoise sky. Cuernavaca cathedral stood out a brilliant pink while the new white villas with their colourful gardens were washed with the golden glow.

Our friends had a house in Cuernavaca and it seemed a good idea to stay with them for a while to get an idea of where we would eventually live. We drove down a long country road cut through a wood. Small houses were built among the trees; an occasional large gateway showed that a bigger house was inside the grounds. Presently we stopped at a pinkish house built on the roadside with a gateway into a garden at the side.

I heard exclamations of excitement from Archie as he made for the garden. Surrounding the house was the formal garden, green lawns with odd built-up flowerbeds of pinkish brick grouped round an old fountain. Beyond was what would have been woods in England, but which here was indisputably jungle. Banana trees reared their blade-like leaves against the dark green of sapote trees; thick vines festooned the branches. The whole made a perfect drop-curtain for the blaze of colour of the garden when even the leaves of the plants were striped or speckled red and yellow, or purple and green.

The house was falling apart, but attractive, with airy rooms and open terraces. It was not the sort of house that Archie and I were looking for, but it gave us an idea of the way to live in Mexico.

The next day Archie and I got up early and went for a walk. We walked round a corner of the road and the ground dropped away to a completely biblical landscape. Even the tones of the hills were the soft greyish-brown of old engravings and the shapes of the shadows and the rays of light reflecting in the sky were exactly like the old pictures of Bible scenes. We walked until we were hungry, and on our way back up the hill to the house we noticed that the road was overhung with different shades of bougainvillea. Purple, scarlet, soft salmon pink, crimson, palest lilac, all were massed together so that not a leaf could be seen. Yet on our way down the road our attention had been so focused on the view that we had not seen even a blink of all that colour.

We found the house was locked. Our friends did not get up till noon; the maid had gone to the market. A locked house does not present much difficulty to Archie. He tried to climb over the big gate. The gate creaked and began to fall to pieces. We did not want to destroy someone else's gate. We thought for a while. Roger, the son of the house, aged eighteen months, watched us with a slightly cynical expression on his face. We walked up to the end of the garden. There was the drain to be negotiated and a thick fence of vines twisted together. We walked back to the gate. Roger watched us. The windows were securely barred or covered with screening. The best bet seemed to be to climb up the stone pillar of the gate, set into an earth wall. A bush with broad rough-looking leaves grew around it. Archie started to climb up. A woman walked by. She seemed entertained. It did look peculiar to see foreigners climbing over people's gates. She said something to me as I started to get a foothold. I could hardly understand her accent. It was something about plants. I followed Archie over into the garden, making full use of the bush as a hand hold.

Roger watched us. The woman watched us. Several other people, picturesque in their white clothes and huge hats, the women with the graceful rebozos, watched us. Suddenly Archie yelled and began to rub his arm violently. I felt an intense burning sensation in my hands. Soon my arms and bare legs burned and stung madly. Great white welts appeared. The onlookers obviously felt it was bad manners to laugh, but their brown faces twitched as they shook their heads and explained that that particular plant with broad rough-looking leaves was poisonous to the touch. Archie and I thanked them bitterly, trying to remove the tiny barbs which, finer than hairs, were sticking all over our hands.

Roger continued to stare at us.

Chapter 10
Mean Altitude

Archie and I are quick learners. We soon learned the rudiments of living in the tropics. First of all the fact of living in the tropics is a perfect excuse for doing no work, becoming extremely peculiar or having no responsibilities. In Mexico City the excuse is the height, the famous *altura* with which we grew so familiar. Cuernavaca is three thousand feet lower, but is still five thousand feet above sea-level, so the *altura* can be dragged in by the scruff of the neck. But a better excuse is the tropics. There is no denying that one is in the tropics anywhere between the Tropic of Cancer and the Tropic of Capricorn. It is all printed on the map. One may freeze at eleven thousand feet or stew at sea-level, it is all the tropics and in the tropics anything may happen.

We learned that malaria lurked in the *barrancas*, the deep canyons that divided Cuernavaca longitudinally, cut by the streams sweeping down from the mountains. Dysentery was invisible. The water was undrinkable. In between bouts of malaria or dysentery, there was that mysterious disease know as Mexican stomach, which was a general feeling of misery.

We were also told that it would be impossible to live anywhere except in a fairly expensive villa because of the various insects that lived in the walls. We said we knew what they meant, bed bugs. Oh dear no, bed bugs indeed! Of course there would be bed bugs. No, far worse things like Black Widow Spiders (one died immediately), *vinagrillos* (absolutely deadly), red scorpions (or sometimes it was the brown, grey or black which were the ones without remedy). We gathered that even if we survived all the insects, unless we lived in a house with a gardener and a large staff, the house would be broken into night after night and we should lose even our three suitcases and rucksack and the typewriter. Also if ever Archie were away, I could not stay alone in a house—I was never clear whether the gardener could protect me or not. The Indians all carried knives and of course everyone knows what Indians are like. I, of course, did not, having only just arrived, but I could take the word of the old residents that the certainly were.

It always sounds a good idea to take the advice of people who know a place. We had survived a war and air raids, but we knew nothing about the tropics. We thought there must be something in all this scare-mongering. We shook out our shoes every morning before putting them on; we boiled the water, we began to despair of finding a house that was within our means. We certainly could not afford to take one with gardener and staff of servants. We took long walks searching for somewhere to live.

It soon became clear that there was something in this tropics business. We should have to live in Cuernavaca itself, although preferably on the outskirts. Immediately one left the bricks and mortar area, one was plunged into the wildness of the countryside with a few mud cottages scattered here and there. Neither Archie nor I minded the idea of living in an adobe cottage, but it was clear that there were drawbacks to living without light and the only water a stream a quarter of a mile distant. Again, the idea of living among the rich foreign residents, even if we had had the money, was still more repellent.

There was no reason why we should have decided to live

in Cuernavaca except that there seemed to be no other place to live. We wanted to be near Mexico City but not to live in such a cold climate. Cuernavaca has a superb climate and is only fifty miles way with buses and turismos every half-hour. There were other places we longed to visit, Mazatlán on the Pacific coast, Oaxaca in the south, but they were places miles away from Mexico City and completely out of the world. I had to be in touch with agents and publishers; Archie hoped to pick up an occasional journalist job. We thought we had a better chance of making a living by being in touch with the world.

One day we found a group of small houses just outside Cuernavaca. They were well-built, villa-ish little houses, with two room, a kitchen and a bathroom. There was a big sun terrace back and front, and they were built high off the road with a good view. The price for rent unfurnished was eight dollars a month.

This was reasonable enough. In fact it seemed too reasonable. We felt there must be something wrong with the house. The only other objection was that the houses were dull. Also we were not too anxious to live in a self-contained little community. However, we decided that it would be worth buying the minimum of furniture to rent at that price.

Then our friends decided to spend a few months in the States and offered to rent us their place. We explained that we could only afford to pay eight dollars a month and they had better look out for more paying tenants. However, it turned out that renting their house was not easy. There were two wild Bedlington terriers who lived in a sort of corral in the garden and who could not be allowed loose for an instant because they ran away and killed chickens. These dogs had to be looked after. The maids were going away also, which mean a great deal of housework in a large house, and also the yearly invasion of bed bugs had started, luckily not in the house, but in a small house in the garden. Archie said he would clear up the bed bugs and I said I would train the dogs. In between times we could look around for a house.

Archie liked Mexico from the first. I like Vera Cruz and my first glimpse of Mexicans, but then I was attacked with violent homesickness. There was enough resemblance to Spain to remind me of Spain and I could not get away from it. I admit that I did not try. I spent hours in Mexico City with Spanish refugees, who were full of complaints. Not complaints because of their difficulties with committees, but bitter complaints because Mexico was not Spain. I realized that they were being unreasonable, but I could sympathize with them. I was also disappointed that Mexico was not Spain.

And I was depressed by the Mexicans. I thought the Indians were charming, but so wrapped in some strange mysticism of their own that they were entirely unapproachable. I resented this after the friendly Spanish people, who feel superior to all other races and therefore have a kindly tolerance for their fellow men. I understood very little of the years of suppression and misery that the Indians have suffered and did not realize that they have been forced to withdraw into this mystic world of their own, but I understood that people have a right to live as they please and I would have accepted the aloofness of the Indians more easily if they had not been so gloomy. A glimpse of a crowd of Indians at the market or in the *zócalo* gave me the impression that some terrific recent calamity had befallen the population. An Indian *fiesta* depressed me more than an air raid. They stood around in the easy attitudes of those who wait for eternity, staring straight before them. Occasionally someone let off a rocket, the only merit of which was the noise. A few more animated participants climbed up the church steeple and banged on the bells with hammers.

I had also the mistaken idea that Mexico was a free nation run for the people of Mexico. I suppose in reality there are few countries with such obvious contrasts between rich and poor. The squalor and poverty strike a European even more than an American, because usually the American has passed through the southern states of his own country and has some idea of what stark poverty is like. It shocked me to see legless beggars and undernourished children squatting beneath a magnificent new building in Mexico City while the streets were jammed with expensive cars, while aged crones, practically held together by their *rebozos*, searched the piles of rubbish for odds and ends to sell. In so-called civilized countries the poor are decently hidden.

Mexico a free nation? Sure it is free. It is as free as the United States and its own politicos will allow. If Mexico is not being cramped by the United States, it is being robbed by its own politicos.

I suppose I had a preconceived idea that life in Mexico would be like in Spain in 1936, '37, before we grasped the extent of German intervention, when the rebels seemed just a handful of tiresome generals, when the people were happy. In those days people walked the streets with broad smiles, slapping each other on the shoulders and crying '*Somos todos iguales*', 'We are all equal'. Of course they were mistaken, but it was swell while it lasted. I think I unconsciously imagined Mexico would be like that.

I did not breathe a word of my feelings. Archie noticed

that I was occupied with refugees and seemed restless. I was always dashing up to Mexico City to see committees and try to do something about a children's colony. It was soon apparent that the Spanish refugees had removed not only themselves but their prejudices to Mexico. There were the same antagonistic groups, the same bickering, the same lack of co-ordination. We gave up hope of starting a children's colony.

Archie sat in the sunshine and loved Mexico. I loved the climate. We had been a month without any of the dire happenings that had been prophesied. We had no malaria, dysentery, no stomach upsets. We did not notice the *altura*. We did not even seem affected by the tropics.

We tried to live as economically as possible to make our reserves last while we found out how to live. We had about two hundred and fifty dollars, some of which was borrowed and had to be returned. With rent at eight dollars a month we reckoned that we could save enough money on food to keep us for a time. The food was utterly different from European food and later we were able to live more economically. Avocado pears, luxuries in Europe, were as cheap as tomatoes. Pineapples cost less than oranges when in season. Potatoes were dear and green vegetables scarce and poor. It took some time to get adjusted and we seemed to have a great many chicken liver omelettes because I could not find tender meat. I was relieved to find the stories that bread is non-existent in Mexico were nonsense and that we need not live exclusively upon tortillas, which seemed to me the last word in dreariness. I would as soon chew pieces of flannel. We thought we were being very careful over our food budget, but later we began to understand better how to eat in Mexico and, what is more, how to survive it.

We got plenty of exercise training the Bedlingtons. They were without exception the most idiotic dogs I had ever seen. They looked awful because the climate did not suit their fur, which hung limply in dingy curls. They were hysterical, they fawned, they jumped up with muddy paws, they were dying for affection, they were violently jealous of one another. However, we trained them to come for walks without the leash; we trained them to come when they were called (that was hard because we never felt like calling them); we trained them to run around the garden free of their corral. We were embarrassed because the neighbours thought they were sheep.

After a month and a half of feeling extremely well physically, Archie said to me, 'I wonder why people make all this fuss about ailments here. It seems to be a kind of disease in itself.'

'It must be the tropics,' I replied.

Chapter 11
Wrong Side of the *Barranca*

We settled down to get used to Mexico and to try to find a cottage more picturesque than the little houses on the wrong side of the *barranca*. It was Mrs Hartley who used that expression. She was horrified when she heard we were considering those homes for an instant.

'My dears,' she said, her bosom swelling, 'you simply can't live on the wrong side of the *barranca*.'

'Why not?' we asked, the little houses suddenly seeming more desirable.

'After all, we British have to keep up some appearances,' said Mrs Hartley.

Mrs Hartley kept up appearances. She was a magnificent-looking woman of sixty, with snowy hair and a pink and white complexion. Mr Hartley gave an impression of an immense scholarly reserve. He was a little man with a white moustache and a love or roses. The Hartley mansion stood back by itself on a slope covered with banana trees. At least the slope had been originally covered with banana trees, but Mr Hartley had made an old English rose garden in the middle of it. Bunches of rotten bananas fell disconcertingly among roses that flourished magnificently. There was also a Dutch garden, a sugar plantation, a coffee plantation, two swimming-pools, and sweep upon sweep of lawn. The seed had been specially imported from England and during the dry season a hundred whirling water jets kept the turf green. The Hartleys took afternoon tea under an aged pine. The butler brought it out on silver trays, Georgian, not Mexican, silver trays.

The tropics . . . the Altitude . . . the Hartleys.

We had been determined not to meet the Hartleys. Everyone spoke of them with bated breath. 'Haven't you met the Hartleys? Oh, but you must.' ('Must we?' we thought grimly). Mrs Hartley saw to it. She saw to so many things. She swooped down on us as we walked across the *zócalo*.

'I hear you want a house,' she said. 'I know just the very thing.'

Mrs Hartley always knew just the very thing. It was practically impossible to be in need of anything in Cuernavaca without Mrs Hartley knowing exactly what one wanted.

We thanked her. We had a house. We need not trouble her at all.

'Trouble?' said Mrs Hartley. 'Good Heavens, it is no trouble. A little friend of mine is just leaving her house—so sad, the husband, you know—and it is just the thing for you both. The poor girl is upset and I want to do all I can.'

'The husband died?' we asked politely.

'Died? My dears, far worse. He just left her stranded. Of course, we all do what we can. I promised I would rent the house for her. It is a bargain, only two hundred dollars a month.'

'Two hundred dollars? You mean pesos?' we said.

'No, no. Dollars. After all, the poor girl has to live.'

'Yes, of course,' we murmured.

'I can sell you the furniture too,' went on Mrs Hartley, warming up. 'I am storing it for her, but it would be much better to sell it all. Start afresh, that's what I say.'

'Thank you,' we said, moving on. 'We are all fixed up for the moment.'

On our way home we were waylaid by Mrs Willoughby-

Houghton. Mrs Willoughby-Houghton was the widow of a British member of the Royal Household, and she never failed to point out that she was entitled to two rooms and a kitchen in Hampton Court Palace. 'Not that I would care to live right on the Thames,' she would say, 'but it is nice to know that if ever I have to return to the Old Country I am entitled to my own little nest.'

'I hear you want a house,' said Mrs Willoughby-Houghton.

'Not exactly,' we explained. 'We are fixed up for the moment—'

'I have something that would suit you perfectly ,' said Mrs Willoughby-Houghton. 'A real bargain and only on the market by an unfortunate circumstance. Not that there weren't faults on both sides, you know, but least said soonest mended. Anyway, the poor girl has to leave, she hasn't a bean. She asked me to rent the house for her. She only wants a hundred dollars. I shall store her furniture, although Heaven knows I haven't much room in my tiny little place. You might like some of the furniture too.'

'Do you mean that house to rent at two hundred dollars?'

'Two hundred dollars?' Mrs Willoughby-Houghton turned pale beneath her parchment skin. 'It's that Hartley woman! I knew it. So she is after it too, is she? That's just like her. Pretending to be a friend of the poor girl and all the time just trying to make something out of her. It's a shame.'

'She sounded as if she wanted to help,' said Archie.

'Help! And what do you think she would be getting out of it? Two hundred dollars indeed. The old place isn't worth two hundred pesos. I suppose she offered to sell the furniture too.'

'She did say something about the furniture,' we said.

'I think it is disgusting,' said Mrs Willoughby-Houghton. 'She just sits there grabbing away at everything. A commission on this, a commission on that. It makes me sick. She is mixed up in all the shady business in this town. How do you think they manage to keep up a big place like theirs? Robbery, that's what I call it.'

'She calls it robbery,' said Archie thoughtfully as we watched the thin, white-haired figure striding up the street.

'Archie,' I said, 'I think we will be in Cuernavaca, but not of it.'

We found the cottage as we walked through the woods behind the garden. We removed a bush, parted some vines, and there it was.

It was covered with straggling roses and obscured by banana trees and high weeds. The main room was built of adobe, but there had been a brick section added. The door was open and we went in. Spider-webs festooned the rotten beams; the windows were broken; a doorway led into a smaller room, hardly more than a closet, and yet another door opened into a bathroom. It was a real bathroom with a wash-basin, toilet and a high built-in bathtub with a shower. Outside the front door there was a narrow porch running the length of the house with a kitchen across one end. Everything was falling to pieces, but Archie has a passion for putting things together.

We set to work. First we cleared away the weeds and discovered that the cottage was set in a little clearing overshadowed by one great tree and surrounded by coffee bushes growing under zapote trees. We had learned that zapotes were a green fruit with a delicious black pulpy inside. Every now and then one would fall from the loaded branches with a squashy thud.

We cut back some of the roses and whitewashed the

cottage. We colour-washed the outside beams a soft pinkish-brown and painted the doors and woodwork a bright cerulean blue. We whitewashed the inside and coloured the beams the same pinkish-brown, which exactly matched the rough tiled floor.

It was difficult to discover the owner of the place but eventually an aged man appeared who said he could act for the owner. He agreed to allow us to rent it for six dollars a month. He was entranced when he saw all we had done and offered to pay for all the whitewashing.

In the attack of bed-bugs, a number of pieces of old furniture had been thrown out to be burned. The little house had been free of bugs, but the landlady, in a mistaken but kind moment, had allowed an Indian family to use it during the wet season. Consequently, everything in the house had been infested. Archie had cleared them out by continuous fumigation. Primed with his success, he tried to reclaim some pieces of furniture. He managed to salvage enough to start making one chair out of two old ones, throwing away the most bug-infested parts and soaking the remaining wood in gasoline. He made a table, a closet, and several sets of shelves. By buying wood and one or two necessary pieces of furniture, we found ourselves equipped. We spent about six dollars. The entire painting of the house and furniture cost us two dollars. I made curtains out of the local cotton, which is hard wearing and can be had in glorious colours. I chose a yellow ground with brick and black cross stripes. With bed covers and cushions, it cost me a dollar. We painted the inside furniture and the inside doors a bright canary yellow to give light to the otherwise dark interior. We figured that equipping the whole house, including some expensive items like aluminium for the kitchen, cost us around twenty dollars.

When we got a moment we tackled the garden. It was virgin soil with a vengeance. We bought a load of sand for half a dollar and covered the earth round the house to make an outdoor patio. We dug up some big flower-beds and robbed all our friends' gardens. This was not so destructive as it sounds. Practically everything 'takes' from slips, and we simply walked around picking branches of coloured leaves and stuck them in our flower-beds. It reminded me of small girls making make-believe gardens in the sand. Only our garden became permanent.

We were still in the big house while we worked. We were glad to be there for the end of the rains. Our cottage would be delightful for the hot, dry season; the trees would provide shade and coolness, but we thought it was better to stay in the big house until the violent storms were finished.

Some of the storms were terrific. The water poured through the cracks in the roof and beat in through the doors and windows. One evening, just before our friends went away. There was an especially heavy storm. We were impressed by the solid sheets of water that sluiced down from the sky. Suddenly a wave swept through the formal garden, broke gently down the steps, and lapped into the house. It was followed by more waves, until the whole ground floor was awash. We ran about with mops and pails, but the water was nearly knee-deep. Archie and I staggered out into the storms to find the source of the water. We discovered, thanks to the vivid flashes of lightning, that the well-meaning gardener had planted the irrigation ditch, especially dug to carry off excess water, full of pretty flowers.

'Why,' said Archie, 'do Mexicans build their houses below water level?'

We grew used to the storms. They never started before eight o'clock and lasted only an hour or two. It was an hour or so of intense drama. Archie was supremely happy. He adores bangs and crashes and secretly even enjoys air-raids. In the tropical thunderstorms he could give full rein to his enjoyment without feeling that anyone was getting hurt. Less than a year out of Spain, I was still at the stage where a sudden loud bang made me instinctively look for a wall to cower against, but I did enjoy the lightning.

Francesca had also found a house in Cuernavaca. She used different methods from ours. Instead of parting the leaves in the jungle, she stood on the top of a roof and looked about her. Her eye lighted on a small hill-top in the middle distance.

'There,' she said, dramatically, 'That is where I want to live.'

She walked to the hill-top and found a house to rent. It was an old ranch-house set in its own grounds, with a screen of tall trees and a perfect view of the volcanos. Everyone who saw it told Francesca how lucky she was.

'Just want we were looking for,' they said. They had never thought of climbing up onto a roof and deciding just like that.

Francesca had a wonderful time furnishing the *rancho*. Her idea weas to take paying guests to help out with the living expenses. We were to be the first visitors the moment we could tear ourselves away from doing up our cottage, but not paying of course. We suggested that Francesca must be firm with her friends. Francesca said that she would never expect her friends to pay for anything. We had doubts about Francesca ever making a financial success out of her guest house.

We were delighted that Francesca had found something

to do that would amuse her. She was one of those people who need occupation, and yet, at the same time, it was difficult to stop her rushing herself to death. She had tremendous enthusiasm and would soar to a pitch of frantic excitement and then crash back to earth in a violent depression. She was the bravest person about her health we had ever met. She was very sick much of the time and would face some real crisis with the utmost calm. But small details would upset her. She was a mass of contradictions. He hated to be alone and she hated having people continually around her. She would change her mind completely twice a day and it was hard to keep up with it. Only João was imperturbable. He was devoted to her and knew exactly how to manage her. We thought the guest house was a good idea. It would keep Francesca busy; it would give João an occupation; there would always be people around; João could look after Francesca if she were sick; I could always be counted on to look after the guests and the food in a crisis. We knew that nothing would prevent Francesca giving everyone far too much for his money but she might as well give it away that way as any other. Francesca had less sense of property than an anarchist.

So we had found a cottage and Francesca had found a *rancho*. We were settled in Mexico for at least six months. There was no more wondering where we should go an what we should do. The *Iberia* went back to Germany. The next Hamburg-Amerika sailing, the *Orinoco*, came to Vera Cruz. She could not get back.

England declared war on Germany on the 3rd of September 1939.

Chapter 12
Life on $28 a Month

We seemed strangely remote from war. The relief of getting out of the atmosphere of the war of nerves had been so great that we began to feel that there might never be a war. We did not see the Russo-German pact as subtle encouragement to Germany to go ahead so much as a result of the persistent sabotaging of good relations between the U.S.S.R. and Great Britain by Great Britain's leaders. We were so used to these leaders' complacency under provocation by Germany that it was a surprise when Great Britain decided to honour her obligations to Poland, even though the honouring was done on paper only. We could not see how Britain could be led into a real war with her present leaders, a large number of whom were even pro-Hitler. The long deadlock that followed showed that the leaders still could not make up their minds.

'One day Hitler will decide all their problems for them,' said an American journalist, 'and then it will be too late.'

We decided that until those in Europe could make up their minds, we would not get too worked up about the war. There were people who went rushing around screaming that there was a war on, WAR, in capitals. We said that there had been a war going in since 1914. It was shifting a little nearer home, that was all. And European statesmen were doing all they could to shift it far away, as far East as they could manage. Mrs Willoughby-Houghton said that she personally would like to see all Germans wiped out, men, women and children.

'There can never be peace so long as there are any

Germans left alive,' she declared dramatically and she cut dead all the Germans she knew, whether they were Hitler refugees or Nazis.

Mrs. Hartley was not so dogmatic.

'One can't blame the Germans entirely,' she said, patting her neat linen jacket and tucking away a wisp of white hair. 'After all, we British were very foolish after the Great War. We should have gone right on fighting to Berlin itself.'

There was an awkward moment at Angel Brady's tea-party. Angel was Irish and therefore no involved in her neighbours' quarrels. She had friends among the English, American and German colonies, and several of them came to tea. The English were already seated, tea-cups in hand, when three German refugees walked in. The English rose in a body, put down their cups with military precision and walked out.

Angel was a kindly soul. She had never been to Ireland, which made her decorate her normal American accent with strange Irishisms never heard of in the Emerald Isle. She could not have children so she satisfied her thwarted mother instinct by figuratively adopting all the coloured races.

'The poor craylures,' she would cry, 'and they the same as you or I, save for their skins.'

Angel would not admit degrees in anything. Just as everyone with a drop of coloured blood was a 'nigger' to many Americans, all coloured people were suppressed and downtrodden to Angel. She was more colour-conscious than the average southerner. She was so determined that the poor things were suffering agonies of self-consciousness because of their complexions that she became violently self-conscious herself and so brightly cheerful that everyone became embarrassed. It was difficult for her in Mexico, where the average Indian is intensely proud of being an Indian. He will explain that he has not a drop of white blood, '*Soy puro indio*,' and he is proud of it. Angel continued to pity him, not because he was poor or diseased, but because he was coloured.

When Archie and I are with Americans we often find ourselves up against this colour question. Never having lived in or even visited the British colonies, we have little colour-consciousness. It just seems crazy to us to object to anyone just because he is coloured. It seems equally crazy to have to love any one like a brother just because he *is* coloured.

We found ourselves knowing several people in a casual way. We liked Mrs Hartley, Mrs Willoughby-Houghton, Angel, and other residents whom we met, but we never felt we wanted to get very well acquainted with them. There were certain people in Cuernavaca whom it was part of Cuernavaca to know. Rosa King, author of *Tempest Over Mexico*, best-seller about the 1910 revolution, is an integral part of Cuernavaca. Few tourists pass through without talking with the dignified elderly lady who sells them the best huaraches in the town. The tourists get more than a pair of shoes. They get a charming smile and the definite feeling that they are the personal friends of someone who was actually at the battle of Cuernavaca. We saluted Rosa King because we felt we were all professionals together. We had been successful hotel-keepers and she was a most successful seller of shoes. It was a relief to find someone who actually did a job of work.

We moved into our house. It seemed like heaven to be in a house of our own again. Although we did not have that house precisely to ourselves.

There were the strangest scuffling noises in the roof,

between the decayed beams and the roof itself. We thought of rats or even of blue mice. We had seen a blue mouse in an out-house of the big house. It was larger than an ordinary mouse, with huge transparent ears and it was a distinct navy blue. We asked our friends' gardener and he laughed and said it must be *tejones*. He brought us a tame *tejón* to show us—a pretty little animal that seemed to be a cross between a rat and a squirrel.

It was all very well for *tejones* to be pretty but they were a nuisance in the roof. There was quite a family. Papa would come home apparently drunk and we could hear him picking his way carefully across the beams. Then he would start in on the family. Wham, wham, clonk, wheee. Little *tejones* scampered away in all directions squeaking and shrieking. After a while Papa settled down and snored. Small *tejones* scuffled back to bed and whimpered themselves to sleep.

Otherwise it was marvellous to be in our own small house. We had tried hard to be enthusiastic about Francesca's *rancho*, but we had been terribly jealous. Now that we had our own cottage we could truthfully say how much we liked her place. We did not envy her her fine terrace with a view of the volcanoes when we had all our meals in the shade of banana trees. I did my laundry under a zapote tree with a background of coffee bushes, and clothes were dry in twenty minutes. The garden looked as it had been planted years and the big trees all around gave the whole place a feeling of comfort.

Francesca already had two guests, and the fame of her cooking was spreading through the grapevine of Cuernavaca.

I am certain that no prison could have had a better underground channel of information than Cuernavaca. The more malicious the news, the quicker it spread. The focal point was a group of Harpies of varying ages. Around them fluttered a flock of white-headed Vultures of both sexes, eagerly glancing from side to side for a juicy but thoroughly dead morsel.

The Harpies and the Vultures were all foreigners, and the only interesting point about them was their attitude to Mexico. On the one hand, Mexico held no interest for them except in a monetary sense. For various reasons they lived in the country, and as a general rule they made their living out of the country. The degrees of their living varied from scratching around in the dust of their richer acquaintances, running small businesses, running bigger businesses, being connected with or owning really big businesses.

Their wealth and comforts were bound up in Mexico. They battened on other foreigners and less astute Mexicans. They numbered among their acquaintances (Harpies and Vultures do not have friends) several rich Mexicans, or if the Harpy or Vulture were poor, no Mexicans. In any case they never knew any Indians. Indians were something that hung like a perpetual menace on the horizons of the Harpies and Vultures. The Harpies and the Vultures were scared. They lived in Mexico, they made money in Mexico, but Mexico was too big for them. They only felt safe in a tight little circle in Mexico City or in even tighter circles in small towns like Cuernavaca, where the governor could be relied upon to support them in a crisis. They never knew what they meant by a 'crisis'. They could not formulate the secret terror that hid growling behind the mountains. They simply knew that it was there—a brooding shadow veiled in mysticism, something that was essentially Mexico.

In conversation this terror manifested itself by remarks

about the fecklessness of the Indians; their ineptitude for learning; the hopelessness of trying to do anything for them. It was frantic wishful-thinking. It was such a comfort for a bunch of poor old Vultures to feel that the only people they could not injure were utterly unworthy of injury. It was a comfort to think, during one of those moments after sundown, when the land of Mexico seems to take a deep breath before plunging into darkness, that the intangible danger lurking in the velvet night was feckless, illiterate, and hopeless.

Archie and I never mind living alone and seeing no-one but ourselves. In fact we like it. We are always interested to meet the people of the country we live in, but we are not particularly interested to meet other foreigners. We would have liked to live miles away in the country, but, with the necessity of earning our living, we had to be near so-called civilization. We thought Cuernavaca was ideal because it was big enough to avoid knowing people if one did not wish to.

I made it clear that I was working and did not wish to meet anyone. Archie is slightly more gregarious and Francesca is incorrigible. She immediately knew a collection of residents, the Right People, the Wrong People, and just People. It was through Francesca that Archie got a permit and became a teacher. At least Archie got the permit to teach through Mexican friends of his and Francesca found the pupils.

It was a job that suited him perfectly. He likes children, he loves teaching and he has an amazing store of knowledge. He started with a boy of thirteen and was supremely happy wrestling with algebraical problems. The boy was intelligent and, more important, Archie earned five dollars a week. The Johnstones were starting to earn their keep.

Our attitude to living was peculiar. We did not care to live expensively even if we had had the money. We felt we should try to build up a reserve so that we could move to another country if we wanted to, or better still, travel round in the one we were in. We wanted to have a reserve behind us and to earn enough to keep us in a simple way. We did not want to work too hard and we did not want to tie ourselves down.

I considered that my English market had dropped out. It was uncertain how much paper there would be; it was not sure if money could be sent out of the country; it was difficult to gauge the market from a distance in wartime. That meant that I had only the United States, until then a subsidiary market to the English one, and I did not know how to write in American style. I never had an aggressively English style, but I certainly did not know American. I decided that Archie must tide us over while I learned to write and speak American.

Our good fortune was that we had been through the Spanish war. That meant that we considered as a luxury the fact that it was possible to walk into a store and buy something. We had been so short of even essentials that we did not consider it any hardship to have to do without the usual luxuries. I hate having a maid, and however much money I had I would prefer to live in a small house I could run myself. Our cottage cost us six dollars in rent; our food cost us four dollars a week. We found that we could manage to live, including everything, for twenty-eight dollars a month. Archie earned, with one child, twenty dollars a month. That meant that we only had to find eight dollars out of our reserve.

Living on twenty-eight dollars was not easy in

Cuernavaca. There are places in Mexico where it would be more than ample, but Cuernavaca is a foreign section where prices are scaled accordingly. The average foreigner paid far more because he like imported food. We knew that to live cheaply we must eat the food of the country. That does not mean that we had to eat chiles with everything. I have never been able to make up my mind whether the Mexicans eat chiles because *tortillas* are so dull, or they eat *tortillas* because chiles are so hot. *Tortillas* are like round pieces of flannel with about as much flavour. They are made of ground, soaked corn called *masa*, well and truly handled and patted until each round is wafer-thin. It is then put on a hot grid, where it swells and writhes, until it is turned over and finally deposited, still limp but warm, on a huge pile of other *tortillas* wrapped in a cloth.

There are things to be done with *tortillas* which make them edible, and we did them. We stuffed them with cooked meat and stewed them in tomato juice; we made *enchiladas*, crisping the *tortillas* first in hot oil, then dipping them in a green sauce made from ground cherries and serving them with strips of meat inside and cheese sprinkled on top. I discovered that the *masa*, bought for one cent, could be fried with eggs and bacon and make a meal for four. It could also be used as pie crust. The bacon was Mexican bacon, which was excellent, but most foreigners preferred the imported at nearly twice the price.

We drank Mexican coffee at 12 cents and pound; we gave up tea, which was imported and therefore dear; Archie smoked cigarettes which cost him 10 cents a packet of 15; he drank rum at 30 cents a bottle and a bottle lasted him two weeks. We gave up drinking in the local café, which was a real hardship because it gave an excuse for a stroll after supper into town. The Universal was a dreary café, right on the side-walk with cars practically brushing the table, but it was the only café in town where one could sit outside and watch the people. We became quite attached to the Universal. Archie accepted the noise and the dust and I was controlled about memories of our café on the beach in Spain.

Archie got another pupil. Ten dollars a week! We relaxed our rule about the Universal first of all. The dollars a week meant that we could give up dipping into our reserves. We could sit in the Universal when we felt like it. We could afford sauté potatoes every day. Archie could buy a pair of new cotton trousers. I could get some next blouses and skirts.

Clothes were no problem in Cuernavaca. Archie wore linen (relics from France) or cotton trousers and bright-coloured shirts; I wore cotton skirts made from the lovely Indian cottons in stripes and checks, and white blouses. We found a Spanish shop in Mexico City which sold *alpargatas*, the Spanish rope-soled shoes with canvas uppers and no heels. I never liked Mexican *huaraches* with their tortured strips of leather cutting into one's toes. The *alpargatas* cost 20 cents, but they wore out in a couple of months. Archie found some leather *huaraches* in the market which were fairly well made and which cost him 80 cents, but he kept those for best.

So in three months we were managing to keep ourselves without counting on my writing. (Archie's ambition is for my writing to keep us). We had our cottage, a few sticks of furniture, some new clothes, and no dependents. We decided that we had had our lesson in Spain. We could not collect things; we would own nothing of value except the typewriter. We would not even have a dog.

So Capulin moved in. Capulin was a black cat belonging to our neighbours. We had made friends with him while we rented their house. They had assured us that he was a wild cat and did not like anyone. He seemed to like us. When we moved to the cottage, Capulin moved too. He was a pleasant, dignified cat and no fool. He put in an occasional appearance at the big house, so that no one knew he had moved out. In that way he was fed by both of us.

Chapter 13
A Drumming Noise

A charming couple called Jane and John rented the house next to the big house. Jane was as pretty as a flower, with delicate white skin, dark curling hair, huge dark eyes. She looked like a delicate piece of china. And she was completely tough. She had the most exquisite legs and knew it. John was huge, red-headed, and obstinate. He determinedly wrote plays. The pair of them were highly entertaining, and we loved them.

They loved us and they loved Cuernavaca. The only thing they did not love was the police band. No one could love the police band. It seems that bugle-blowing is a passion in Mexico. Unlike most passions, no one ever attains perfection. The Cuernavaca police band was terrible.

We thought that they were learning and should at least be respected, if not encouraged, but we have since found out that the police band has been practising for years. Unfortunately it chose the wrong times and places to practise.

At five o'clock every morning the Cuernavaca police band marched forth. Everyone in Cuernavaca could hear the noise in varying degrees. The band marched down streets and up streets and we all knew the off notes and mistaken beats by heart. But we in Calle Humboldt had never really known the police band. It had never marched down our street.

One morning we were awakened by a shattering noise. The house was shaking and a terrible drumming vibrated in our ears. It grew louder until we thought something would burst. The a thin, reedy sound broke above the clamour. It was just off the note. We recognized the police band at close quarters. They marched twenty strong past our windows, blowing lustily and drumming madly. The noise was terrific. It would have been maddening at any time but at five in the morning it was devastating. Jane and John complained bitterly. We said we thought it was only fair that our street get it once in a while. Luckily there were many streets in Cuernavaca.

There is something about the Calle Humboldt that is attractive. Jane and John liked it, our friends liked it and we liked it. So did the police band. It was undoubtedly the most charming street in Cuernavaca. The police band marched down it every morning.

After a week our nerves were shattered and we were wrecks. John said he would put a stop to it. He would show the police band. I suggested we might go to the police and ask them to use another street. That would have been the obvious solution in Spain. The old residents laughed me to scorn. Everyone in Mexico knew just what Mexican police were like. It was no good asking them anything. They were only interested in bribes. They hated foreigners anyway, so they were probably doing it just to annoy. It would be useless to ask the police.

We left it to John. The next morning the band came gaily down the street. I got up and rushed over to the big house to see what John would do. As the band drew alongside, fairly bursting themselves with noise, there arose a fearful howling and crashing. John appeared on the terrace beating an iron tray with a hammer and yowling at the top of his voice.

The band marched on unperturbed. Suddenly John lifted up his voice in a perfect imitation of a bugle off-note. It rang out clear and utterly out of tune above the noise of the police band. The effect was startling. The noise quavered and broke. The band shuffled to a stop. There was utter silence.

John disappeared. The band gathered in a little bunch to discuss the matter. There was whispering. Then two policemen walked determinedly up to the door of John's house and knocked. The sound echoed like the crack of doom.

There was no answer. John and Jane were hiding. The maids had not arrived.

The policemen knocked some more. Then they whispered some more. An old woman from a cottage across the way came out and began to fill her apron with stones. I thought she was going to take her revenge on the band at last, but she disappeared again into her cottage with the stones. At last the band formed again into ranks, but its spirit was broken. It shuffled away in silence, a wreck of its former self.

Jane and I were lounging by her swimming pool when the policeman came to arrest John. He was a nervous policeman and he could not take his eyes off Jane's legs. Jane upset him completely by putting on her bathrobe. Her bathrobe was a work of genius. It buttoned tightly round the neck, had long flowing sleeves buttoned at the wrist, hung perfectly straight down in a smock effect and stopped short a few millimetres above the hips. We assured him that John was not in. He went away in a trance.

Shortly after another policeman arrived. He was just as overcome by Jane's legs. He went away.

Jane said, 'This is all wonderful but I can't stay this way for the rest of my life. John must give himself up.'

The third policeman arrested John. Jane and I put on

our best clothes and went to the police station.

The chief of police was an aristocratic looking person. He seemed severe. I explained that I was not in this but that my friends could not speak Spanish. I wished to explain the situation. The chief of police appeared tired. He leaned back and said that he did not wish to make trouble but that when he was in a foreign country he believed at all times in being courteous. There were customs that he deplored in the United States but he never became discourteous. He was sorry we did not like the police band but he thought it was going too far to throw stones at them. I asked him to repeat that. I was sure I had misunderstood. He said even more severely, slightly raising his voice: 'I think it is going too far to throw stones at the police band.'

For a moment I detected a wistful note. I realized how he longed to throw stones at the police band. I said, 'But that is absurd. I saw the whole thing and no one threw any stones. It was not possible because the terrace was screened. The señor could not have thrown stones even if he had found any on his terrace.'

The police chief wearily called a policeman. The man came in carrying a handful of stones to prove it.

'An old woman from across the street saw the stones thrown,' he said.

I remembered the old woman picking up stones. I told the police chief what I had seen. 'Wouldn't it be a good idea to get the old woman here?' I suggested.

The chief of police agreed. We should all come back the next day and confront the witness. John was released.

The old residents said we had been ridiculous. The idea of bothering about witnesses. Of course Mexicans would lie against foreigners. We should have slipped the chief of police half a dollar and the whole thing would have been forgotten. I had probably got John and Jane into serious trouble.

I was worried, but I could not see how any one could have slipped that chief of police anything under a thousand pesos. And even the I had an idea he would have refused it. I tried to point this out, but everyone said nonsense. All Mexican police were corrupt. No Mexican police got their pay. All Mexican police hated foreigners.

We went back the next day. The old woman stuck to her story. She even elaborated it. Not only had John thrown stones but it should be no surprise that John had thrown stones. Any people who got blind drunk every night and rushed round the garden shooting off revolvers might be expected to throw stones.

The situation was getting out of hand. I did not dare translate this to John who was sitting with a scarlet face badly clashing with his red hair. I denied hotly that John and Jane got drunk or shot off revolvers.

'Send one of your men down at once to see if there are any revolvers in the house,' I said. 'It is a fantastic story and the old woman is a liar.'

The chief of police looked at us for a moment and went out of the room. Presently he came back and he looked less severe. He told the old woman to go home. He said, 'And all the señor did was to bang on a tray and scream?'

'He did do a marvellous job of a bugle off-note,' I said. 'That was what stopped them.'

The chief of police's face twitched.

'The old woman was a relation of one of the band,' he explained. 'Her testimony is unreliable. I think we can consider the matter at an end. But another time it would be better to come to me with complaints.'

We thanked him. I felt that something should be done to

celebrate this.

'Do you ever have time to take a drink?' I asked. The señor John would be so glad if you could join us right away.'

The chief of police considered. He would be delighted to have a drink with us. If we would wait ten minutes—

We waited. He fussed with some papers and then said he was ready to go. As we were leaving he called in one of the policemen. He was a member of the band.

'The police band,' said the chief of police firmly, 'is *never* to march down Humboldt again in the early morning.'

He then followed us out and drove up in his car to the Country Club where he insisted on standing us drinks. John and I drank a silent toast—to Jane's Legs.

Chapter 14
Scorpions and *Pulque*

Biscuit moved in. Biscuit was a yellow puppy with every bone showing and sentimental amber eyes. Archie and I considered the situation.

'We don't really want a dog,' I said.

'We certainly don't want a dog,' said Archie firmly. He hates responsibilities and has never forgotten how we were landed with seventy children in Spain, and that we had had to leave Beetle there. Biscuit stood gazing at us. His front legs were knock-kneed and he looked rickety. He screwed up his eyes and his large ears flopped gently. He walked on to the porch and lay down with a rattle of bones.

'If we feed him once we are sunk,' I said. 'He will never go away.'

'He must belong to someone,' said Archie hopefully. We both knew just where Biscuit belonged. An Indian family had been camping in the woods behind our house and their nondescript bitch had had puppies. The family moved and somehow Biscuit had got left. He was about three months old.

'We shall have to decide,' I said. 'If we feed him he is ours.'

Archie sighed.

Biscuit ate his food. He stretched himself and lay down on his back. We sat and watched the fleas chase each other across his pink belly. Archie got up quietly and walked to the town. He came back with flea soap.

After Biscuit was washed he looked beautiful but shattered. His illusions were ruined. He had thought he had found a home with food and comforts and then this happened. He gave us a reproachful look out of his mild eyes and went off into the woods. We were delighted. We had wasted a few cents on soap, but we no longer had responsibilities.

The next day Biscuit returned. His coat was a shining blond and he looked at us deprecatingly. His ears stuck out at right angles and then drooped at the tips. Archie looked at him.

'If those ears straighten out, he will be quite a nice-looking dog,' said Archie, assuming his responsibilities manfully.

Capulin, the black cat who really belonged next door, summed Biscuit up with a disdainful look. Biscuit would be managed. Biscuit thought Capulin was wonderful. He followed Capulin round fairly squinting with admiration. Capulin accepted it as his due.

Lizzie, the remaining Bedlington (one had mercifully died) also decided that our cottage was an ideal home. We had other ideas. We chased her out, we threw stones, we cursed, we beat her with sticks. Lizzie loved us. She simply could not understand that we did not like her.

Roger, our neighbour's son and heir, also had a tendency to wander over to explore the woods round us. He was an amazing child. He had more concentration than most grown-ups and worked for hours with his hands trying to build walls, dams, or castles.

We were less drastic with Roger than with Lizzie, but we managed to persuade him that his own garden was more amusing. Luckily a charming Indian boy called Augustín came to look after the garden. He was soon looking after everything, including Roger.

Apart from occasional incursions by our neighbours our

lives were as routine as can be expected in a country abounding with poisonous insects, fevers, and peculiar diseases. The fevers and diseases seemed to pass us by, but we had our share of insects.

I have never disliked spiders, nor have I any violent reaction to things that crawl or wriggle. We had heard so many scare stories when we first arrived that I really shook out my shoes and jumped when something plopped on the floor in the dark. But after living in our cottage I became indifferent to almost anything.

We killed an average of four scorpions every day. Archie invented our excellent technique. He would fetch his trusty ruler and squash the creature's head. The scorpion would attack the ruler and fall dead on the floor. In this way we saved our white-washed walls from splashes of brown, red, grey, or black, according to the colours of the scorpions. I do not find anything repulsive about scorpions; they are rather decorative and they do not seem to have any intention of attacking anyone. The danger is in finding them in shoes or clothes. Archie went happily walking down the garden in a pair of pants he had not worn for some time with a scorpion posed gracefully on the seat of his pants. It was quite a problem.

It seemed to us that with a reasonable amount of care, there was no need to get stung. I should have been stung one day when I was in the woodshed and my mind was elsewhere. I saw something on the wall and dimly registered that it was something that did not belong there. So I picked it up and threw it out. As it hit the ground it crawled rapidly away and I saw it was a scorpion, about two inches long. I must have picked it up by the body in such way that it was paralysed and cold not jerk its tail over to sting me.

There was a tremendous amount of nonsense talked about the deadliness of scorpions. People loved to tell how deadly they were. Archie tried to find out the mortality rate from scorpion stings in Cuernavaca and he could not hear of anyone having died. There was no doubt that a sting is unpleasant, and the cure, the beloved Mexican injection, was even more drastic than the sting. Augustín, the neighbour's gardener, was stung. He was extremely lofty about it and insisted that dipping his arm in cold water was sufficient. However, in about an hour he could not keep a cigarette between his lips and he looked scared to death. So he went up to La Luz, the big drug store with its sign up to say it was run by 'Dr Caballero, unqualified', where he got his injection. He recovered rapidly, but he suggested that foreigners might suffer more. He considered that a fatalistic attitude towards all noxious insects was the only one to have, and this was certainly true with regard to Roger, who had a passion for poking under stones.

Roger had broken out in red spots which nothing seemed to cure. One day everyone though they were caused by eating butter; then it was eggs; then it was spinach. Dr Caballero gave him bottles of medicine. Roger continued to work doggedly in the garden , but he was still covered with spots.

Augustín had a room in a little house at the end of the garden. In the evenings he would have his friends in for supper. He cooked enchiladas over a brazier and everyone sat around on the ground and talked. One evening his friend Bartolo brought something special. They had a feast and then someone mentioned Roger's hives. Bartolo assured Augustín that his speciality would cure the hives immediately. Roger was perfectly ready to try anything once.

I met his mother a few days later and she was looking delighted.

'Roger's hives are cured,' she said. 'Augustín and Bartolo gave him skunk stew.'

'How wonderful,' I said. 'Are the spots all gone?'

'All gone. It really is a relief.'

'I'm terribly glad,' I said. Then I thought for a moment. Skunk stew? Skunk stew?

'Good heavens,' I exclaimed belatedly. 'Skunk stew!'

That is one of the troubles of living in the tropics. Nothing seems surprising after a while.

Hamilton Rice was much impressed with the skunk stew story. He assured us that there were many similar discoveries that civilized mankind had forgotten. We should all try to get closer to nature.

Hamilton Rice was a long way from nature. He was carefully preserved with thinning curly blond hair. He was in Mexico making a study of folk-songs. He wore exquisite silk shirts and a solar toupee and he had travelled extensively in Europe.

'You know, dear lady,' he said to Angel Brady. 'You are too tender-hearted. Now, Indians are cruel and ruthless and it is no good sentimentalizing about them. They are an inferior race and they know it. Not that they don't have their good points. There is a great deal in the old Aztec civilization that is excellent. But they are all barbarians.'

'Nonsense,' said Angel, swelling visibly. 'That is the worst of you colour-conscious people. You can never get away from all this inferior and superior business. Now I think the Indians have a far better sense of living than the whites.'

'For those who like discomfort,' murmured Hamilton Rice, 'life as the Indians live it might be all right. But to me there is simply no charm in it. And life without charm—well, what is it?'

No one round the table at the Universal seemed to know.

'I must have delightful surroundings,' went on Hamilton Rice. 'So long as I have certain possessions I can always make any surroundings delightful.' He paused.

'What possessions?' asked someone at last.

He beamed. 'I have an early Georgian teapot,' he said with a caress in his voice. 'I cannot bear tea out of any other pot. When it is not in use. I keep it on a little shelf where I can see it from my bed. My eyes can fondle its exquisite curves by the shadow of a candle. I always use candles,' he explained. 'Electric light is so crude. I like my room bright with the softness of candle light. I use a dozen candles in a night. Then I have two little Degas pictures, just trifles the Master must have dashed off, but they please me, they please me. And my books, of course. Such companions.'

'The Indians,' broke in Angel, 'are above such things as mere possessions. They have their souls.'

'They are extraordinarily dirty,' said someone.

'It is simply a different way of looking at life,' said Angel. 'Their bodies may be dirty but their souls are clean.'

'Mexico is ruined by the *mestizos*,' said Hamilton Rice. 'Nothing good ever came out of mixing races.'

'Mexico is saved by the *mestizos*,' declared Angel. 'There is no colour problem any more. Everyone is equal and happy.'

'It is curious that one invariably finds the menial work done by Indians,' said Hamilton Rice. 'According to your theory there should be as many white servants as there are coloured ones.'

'That has nothing to do with colour,' said Angel. 'It is

simply that the Indians are more fitted for that sort of work.'

'Taking of servants,' said Mrs Willoughby-Houghton, who had just joined the party. 'I have just heard from Home and the servant problem is simply terrific. I can't understand what is the matter with the silly girls, throwing away chances of nice homes to earn less in a stuffy office.'

'They like their independence,' said Angel.

'Oh, what nonsense. As if they didn't have their independence in a modern house. Why, all my friends give their girls a full afternoon off every week and very often Sundays as well. In any case, the upper classes in England almost always have a cold Sunday supper so that the girls can get to church in the evening. Independence indeed, they can stay out until ten at night!'

'I would rather work in an office,' said Angel. 'The conditions among the coloured servants in the States—'

'I wonder why coming in at ten is supposed to save the morals of servants,' mused Hamilton Rice. 'Such an odd idea that one cannot fornicate before 10 p.m. Now, I—'

Mrs Willoughby-Houghton stared at him. Angel went on hastily, 'I think the feeling that one is living with one's work must be very trying. I should infinitely prefer to live in even uncomfortable lodgings and to get away from my work every night.'

'Absurd,' said Mrs Willoughby-Houghton, still eyeing Hamilton Rice. 'The girls don't know what is good for them.'

'Well, there are no problems like that here,' said Angel. 'Mexican problems are entirely different.'

'Oh, *here*,' said Mrs Willoughby-Houghton. She had lived in Mexico for fifteen years and nothing surprised her any more. 'Here anything may happen. I have never found a good girl in this country. There is always something wrong. They drink, or take marijuana. And steal! My goodness, how they steal. I though I had found a possible little girl the other day but we couldn't get on. She didn't speak my language.'

'You mean that in the figurative sense, I presume,' said Hamilton Rice.

'Figurative sense?' said Mrs Willoughby-Houghton. 'I mean that the girl couldn't speak English.'

'Mrs Willoughby-Houghton doesn't speak Spanish,' said Angel.

'I do not, and I am proud of it,' said Mrs Willoughby-Houghton.

'Marijuana,' said Hamilton Rice thoughtfully. 'I suppose there must be a lot of the weed about.'

'That and *pulque*,' said Angel. 'They are the scourge of the country.'

'I confess that *pulque* seems a loathsome drink,' said Hamilton Rice. 'I have read that after the juice is extracted from the maguey plant, flavour has to be added to satisfy the chile-ruined palates of the Indians. Anything short of actual poison is use, old *huaraches* are a favourite flavouring, and even the excrement of dogs and horses—'

'Really,' said Mrs Willoughby-Houghton. She began to gather up her belongings. Mrs Willoughby-Houghton invariably carried a number of small packages. She rose and glanced across the street at the *zócalo* with its crowds of country people, white-clothed and big-hatted. 'There is Hiram,' she said. 'I must go. Such a tiring young man and most peculiar. There were some very strange stories about him and that blond woman—one never knows, does one?'

She strode away, her white hair wisping out from under the ornate sun-hat of blue and green straw. Hiram came over and joined the party. He was a tall young man with untidy black curly hair.

'*Pulque*,' Hamilton Rice was saying. 'It acts directly on the nervous system. People do mad acts under the influence of *pulque*.'

'That's not true,' cried Hiram vehemently. 'You are talking nonsense. It is absolutely untrue.'

'Now, now,' said Angel. 'You must admit that people get horribly drunk on *pulque*.'

'Sure they do,' said Hiram. 'But it is a lie to say that people get mad. *Pulque* simply makes them high. They feel wonderful. You know,' he turned seriously to Hamilton Rice, 'you just don't know what you are talking about.'

'Indeed?' said Hamilton Rice stiffly. 'Then I am afraid you must excuse me. Good-bye, Angel.' He rose and walked away, heroically keeping down a tendency to waddle.

Hiram stared after him. 'What is the matter with that guy?' he asked. 'He seems to be sore about something.'

'Well, you were very rude to him,' said Angel.

'Rude? Me? Nonsense. Why, that is absurd. You don't know what you're saying.'

'Some people don't like being told they are half-witted,' said Angel mildly.

'But I only told him the truth,' said Hiram, and he sounded hurt. 'He didn't know what he was talking about. Why, everyone knows that *pulque* is just a soporific. No one could get mad on *pulque*. It's been proved scientifically—'

That night the Mayor of Cuernavaca and the chief of the local police had a *pulque* party. The result was that the policeman was killed and the mayor seriously wounded, not expected to live. Hiram had made a mistake.

Chapter 15
Neighbours, just Neighbours

It was Hiram's own idea that he should become an Idea Man. His second idea was that he should grow a moustache.

Archie and I liked Hiram. Everyone liked him to start with but many people could not face up to the fact that they were illiterate bone-heads; that their whole lives had been lived in the intellectual backwoods; that they were, in effect, mentally deficient.

Hiram was genuinely convinced that people who disagreed with him on any subject were not just wrong but wrong in the head. Unfortunately nearly everyone disagreed with Hiram. Consequently his only faithful friends were his ideas and his moustache; and even that went back on him.

The moustache would not grow. Hiram's vision of a moustache was something to be stroked gently when in the throes of an Idea, something out of which selling lines could be shaken as apples out of a tree. It is difficult to stroke with any careless rapture a growth of stunted down; it is utterly impossible to shake it. There seemed to be no reason why Hiram should not grow a moustache. He was a healthy, husky young man with masses of black curls, jutting eyebrows and long lashes. He probably had hair on his chest. However, the moustache held back and Hiram's ideas with it.

Hiram loved talking. He would talk about anything with absolute authority, but he was fair. He admitted there were a few subjects upon which he was not an authority. He allowed Archie to know how Fleet Street ran newspapers and he allowed me to know something about the Spanish war. Archie was allowed to talk about journalism so long as it was clearly understood that he was confining himself to journalism in Europe. I was allowed to murmur an opinion about politics provided I discussed only Spanish politics.

Archie found that he could glean a certain amount of knowledge from Hiram and Archie is happy as long as he is learning something. I found Hiram charming in his simplicity. We both found that he possessed one priceless gift. He could invariably be made to see when he was being really ridiculous and he found it vastly entertaining.

In some ways Hiram was extremely honest. He had certain convictions, probably acquired during adolescence, which ruled his life, and he was entirely consistent. He had a horror of getting involved in anything socially. He took the attitude that he asked nothing of anyone and no-one should make demands on him. He had perfected this emotional armour until he felt happy only when he was free of all entanglements. He liked women provided they asked nothing and expected nothing. They could not even fix dates a day ahead. Hiram would suddenly feel he was trapped and would refuse to see them again.

Unfortunately Hiram attracted every type of female. Some wanted to reform him, some wanted to mother him, others loved him, many hated him. But they all became violently emotional about him. Instead of developing a hearty distrust of the feminine mind, Hiram was always surprised and hurt over each crisis. He accepted people as he found them, or so he thought. The trouble was that most women found Hiram irresistible.

Hiram liked being with us because he felt at ease. Archie and I were obviously perfectly content with each other, and while I was fond of Hiram I clearly had no designs upon him. Hiram respected Archie for all the qualities that he himself lacked. He was the first to admit that he was unstable. But Hiram believed that there was a possibility that he might make a fortune, while it was clear that Archie, while leading a less complex existence, never would.

The Fortune Idea see-sawed with the Communist Idea. There were times when Hiram, fairly deep in his cups, would sigh for the joys of self-sacrifice and would seriously consider joining the Party. The fact that the Party would probably not seriously consider Hiram did not matter. At these moments Hiram would discourse upon the Proletariat and the merits of the Masses and odds and ends of Marxian phraseology would spring from the stubble of his moustache. (Hiram kept a Handbook of Marxism side by side with the directory of the Chamber of Commerce of Mexico.) One day he said seriously that he could not make up his mind whether to become a millionaire or a Communist. We assured him that he need not worry unduly.

Hiram was not exactly *working* in Mexico. He was waiting for an idea. In the meanwhile he wrote short stories which were brilliant and unsellable. He decided to become an Idea Man shortly after we met him.

His first idea after the moustache-growing effort was to get a friend to write a series of articles on the inner workings of the oil controversy. Hiram had some excellent material and the time element was good. I knew the friend concerned and I told Hiram that he should write the articles himself.

'Robert can't write,' I said. 'He will kill any material, however lively. Please write them yourself.'

'You don't know what you're talking about,' said Hiram. 'Robert is one of my best friends.'

'And so what?' I retorted. 'That doesn't mean that he isn't the most deadly dull creature in Mexico.'

'He used to be an excellent newspaper man,' said Hiram stiffly.

'He probably still is. That doesn't mean he can write.'

'You're talking nonsense. Robert will do these things all right.'

'Why on earth don't you do them yourself?'

'I haven't time. I'm an Idea Man now.'

'You certainly have the lousiest ideas.'

Robert wrote the articles. He killed them dead, one by one. They were never published. Hiram had missed out again.

The Great Idea dawned in spite of the moustache. Hiram came down to see us in a state of violent excitement. He brought with him a little round oily man with shining teeth and sentimental eyes. He was a South American and he thought Hiram was a genius. Hiram respected the little man's judgement. He introduced him as Rafael.

Hiram strode up and down while unfolding the Idea. That meant that plants were crushed underfoot, Capulin fled, abandoning his dinner, which was ground into the gravel, Biscuit rushed away yelping on three legs, a chair was smashed. Hiram was like that.

'It's a cinch,' said Hiram. 'For once here's something that can't go wrong.'

'Ain't he wonderful?' said Rafael.

'Why can't it go wrong?' asked Archie.

'Hell, listen. Do I have to go over it all again? It can't, I tell you. The circulation will be guaranteed by the Mexican state governor before we start a thing. And if you've got circulation you've got—'

'Advertising,' finished Rafael, trotting breathlessly up and down behind the great Idea Man.

'That's all right,' said Archie. 'But why should the state governors buy the paper at all?'

'Why? Because they want to. Because Good Neighbourliness is something everybody wants.'

Archie considered slowly and carefully.

'Do you really think they want Good Neighbourliness?' he asked.

'They will when the see *The Good Neighbour*,' said Hiram with the fondness of a parent.

'Ay,' said Archie with painful concentration.

'*The Good Neighbour*, what a swell title!' said Rafael. 'Hiram's own idea, you know. Hiram has the swellest ideas.'

'Oh, lay off,' said Hiram, but he looked pleased.

'Neighbours, just Neighbours,' murmured Archie.

Later Hiram explained Rafael. Rafael had been born into the world of diplomacy and had stayed in it until he backed the wrong dark horse in a minor revolution. He had brothers or cousins or childhood friends in every embassy, legation, and state department. He loved them as brothers and surprisingly they loved Rafael as a brother, a distant brother. Hiram intended that Rafael should persuade all the embassies, legations, and state departments to order a few thousand copies each of *The Good Neighbour*.

'Rafael will get us in with all the state governors too and fix up everything like that,' he said. 'Besides, his Spanish will come in useful. I tell you, the thing is too easy.'

Archie thought. 'What will you do about money?' he asked.

'Money? We practically don't need money. As soon as I

get a dummy lay-out roughed out, the ads will come in and then we'll have all the money we want.'

'But you must have something to start with. You can't run this on absolutely nothing.'

'Of course we need something. But chicken-feed. I thought that between us—'

Rafael shook his fat cheeks. 'I ain't got a dime,' he said. 'I'm cleaned up.'

Hiram laughed. 'I guess I'm pretty well broke myself. But if I can get around to doing a couple of stories for the slicks, that'll tide us over. Perhaps Archie—'

'I haven't much faith in this whole project,' said Archie.

Hiram launched into a violent defence of his idea. He did not particularly want Archie's money because he knew how little it would be, but he could not bear to have anyone not believe in the Idea. Archie still shook his head. Ideas take a long time to penetrate Archie's dome-like forehead.

'Anyway, we only need dough to tide us over a couple of weeks,' said Hiram. 'The whole thing will be going by then and the ads will be coming in. And then I'll have the money for my stories—'

'When you get the money for your stories, I'll match it,' said Archie.

Rafael grew very red. 'I think you are insulting Hiram,' he spluttered.

'Oh nuts,' said Hiram. 'Archie is just cautious. Actually, Archie, you are just the sort of person I want to help us out. Why don't you come in on this with us?'

Archie considered. 'What exactly would I do?'

'We'll pool all our resources,' said Hiram eagerly, 'and distribute the work. I'll be editor and see about the dummy and the general run of things; Rafael will do the central and state departments and get circulation; you will do the editorial work under me till I go to the States—'

'Why should you go to the States? It'll cost an awful lot of money.'

'We must put this over in the States. Hell, Archie, Good Neighbourliness must include the States.'

Archie's face came as near to registering emotion as it was ever allowed to do.

'Please,' he said. 'Let's save that for the paper. We are all friends here, I hope, and adults. But there is, I admit, a certain community of interest on both sides of the Rió Grande, if we must talk in headlines. Our mission, I take it, is to throw wide open our advertising columns to firms in Mexico who are willing to give American visitors drinks, souvenirs, transport, *huaraches*, and shelter at slightly increased prices and our editorial columns to those officials who are in a position to pay for private boosts out of the public funds.'

Rafael seemed shocked.

'You shouldn't put it like that,' he protested. 'Think of the wonderful opportunity for bringing together the American peoples. Hiram thought of that too, didn't you, Hiram?'

'Sure, sure,' said Hiram.

'There,' said Rafael triumphantly.

'Well,' went on Hiram, 'you, Archie, will be in charge while I am away. I shall take Rafael, of course, to do his stuff with diplomats and officials in the States and you will be in charge of the others here in the office.'

'Others?'

'The advertising men, the space sellers,' said Hiram.

'Oh ay. And who are they?'

'Well, just at the moment we haven't fixed anything. But we'll pick up someone all right. *You* wouldn't care to try your hand at picking up an ad or two, Archie?'

'No,' said Archie.

'What about you, Nancy? Like to try selling space?'

'I would not,' I said.

'All right, all right. The main thing now is the question of immediate expenses.'

'And how do we get paid while we are working?' asked Archie. 'I suppose the advertising men will get paid on commission, but we—'

'We don't get paid,' said Hiram grandly. 'Of course Rafael and I have to raise money for our expenses in the States, but that is different. We three get our cut in the end. Split the profits three ways.'

'Split the profits two ways,' said Archie thoughtfully. 'I'd rather have a salary.'

'What! And lose the chance of making ten thousand pesos?'

'Ay,' said Archie.

'He means he'd rather have a salary,' I explained.

'But think of ten thousand pesos, maybe more.'

'I'm thinking,' said Archie. 'I'd prefer a salary. Paid in advance,' he added.

Later Hiram asked me what I thought of his Idea.

'I'm not sure,' I said slowly. 'I'm not so pessimistic as Archie about everything. There really may be something in it.'

'Whadya mean, something in it? Of course there is something in it. I tell you, you are crazy if—'

'Wait a minute, wait a minute. Don't get so worked up. And mind that rose bush, there, by that outsize shoe of yours. I think there might be a chance of you pulling this off. But not with Rafael.'

'Now what the hell is the matter with Rafael? Just

because a guy is little and fat—'

'I don't care if Rafael is cross-eyed. But I don't like him. I think he is a rat.'

'For God's sake,' said Hiran disgustedly. 'What is the matter with you? You never like my friends.'

'Try taking a good look at them, some day,' I answered.

Chapter 16
Moustache in the Sun

For a week we were busy with our ordinary routine. Archie taught two children every morning from ten to one. I cleaned the house, did the marketing, attended to the laundry, and wrote a chapter. Doing the laundry was pleasant under our conditions. Our *lavadero*, a stone slab with a built-up basin attached to it and a tap of cold water, stood behind the cottage in a small space between the house and the woods. Coffee bushes grew behind it and zapote trees hung their flower-laden branches over it, while humming-birds darted in and out with a whirring of wings that sounded like the grunting of pigs. The water from the tap was lukewarm from the sun on the tank. And at first we had plenty of water.

There was masses of water in Cuernavaca, but it somehow did not reach to all parts. It seemed to depend on whether a *político* was living in one's road. There was a great deal of talk about new pipes, and large sums of money were always being raised, but somehow nothing was ever done. Most people were perfectly resigned to being without water for the greater part of the year. We decided we would try it for ourselves and would see how we got on. We were without water for a few days, and I went up to the Cortez Palace, used as the Town Hall. I walked into an office and told a little man sitting behind a large desk that we wanted water. He told me that the head of the local bank controlled the water supply. I said I had no time to find the head of the local bank on a Saturday afternoon and that I wanted water immediately. I explained that I would come up to the *zócalo* with pails and dip water out of the public fountains if we were not given water. And I would explain to everyone who was interested just why I was having to dip water from public fountains, because the municipality of Cuernavaca would not allow me water in my house.

The little man protested that it really had nothing to do with him. I said I didn't care who it had to do with, I wanted water. I left him pathetically ringing up the head of the bank.

We had water immediately. I found out afterwards that the little man had been perfectly correct. It had nothing to do with him, at least not directly.

He was only the Governor of the State of Morelos.

I was getting ready for Christmas. Usually I do not bother and this year Archie and I were feeling depressed at the thought of last Christmas when we had had such a wonderful time with our refugee children. But there seemed to be a general demand among our friends so we decided to celebrate Christmas by having a house party, using both the cottage and the big house.

Hiram came down bringing a girl with him. An old friend of ours from Spain managed to get away from Mexico City for a few days. The rest of the party consisted of two American girls and an earnest young Slovak. Francesca had her own party for her guests in her *rancho*.

Hiram introduced me to the girl with him as Marjory. She looked vaguely intellectual. She had a pale, transparent skin and straight black hair, which she wore in a bang over her high forehead. She wrote serials for the smaller magazines and was a hard worker. She outmatched her literary agent in business ability and divided her time between New York and Mexico. She had once been married to Hiram.

I liked her immediately. I have a tendency to like efficient people, and Marjory was efficient. She was also attractive.

'I guess I could get hold of some dough,' said Marjory when she heard about the Idea. 'But I'd like to see something concrete first.'

'Hell, Marge,' said Hiram. 'It's all so plain. I've explained everything to you.'

'Have you the dummy prepared? At least that would be something to work on,. I've got to try to sell some sucker this idea.'

'You're wrong, Marge, dead wrong. Whoever puts up money for this paper won't be any sucker. It's a cinch. It can't fail.'

Marjory looked thoughtful. She stared at Hiram and suddenly screwed up her almost black eyes.

'*Darling*, your moustache! It is just catching the light. It's *wonderful*. It's almost glowing.'

'Oh, shut up, Marge. Listen! Let's get on with this business. I tell you—'

'Yes, I know. It's a cinch. But I want something to show this poor boob all the same.'

'Hey, who is this guy, anyway?'

'Oh, just a guy I know. What do you care anyway? His money is all right. But I'm not going to talk him into anything. I'll show him the dope and leave it to him. Then it won't be my fault.'

'What won't be your fault? Say, listen, you've got the wrong idea, I tell you.'

'Hiram, you needn't put over that act with me. Hell, we're married.'

'We're divorced.'

'So we are. Maybe I was thinking of the two other guys. Well, come on, Hiram. Let's have the great Idea all over again. Maybe if I hear it often enough I'll break down and begin to believe in the Brotherhood of the Americas myself.'

We had a hilarious Christmas. It started a day or two before Christmas Day, and no one seemed to want to leave, so it went right on over New Year's Day. Everyone seemed to be having a wonderful time, and everyone seemed filled with the Christmas spirit of goodwill and kindness towards each other. The members of the house-party became so affectionate that it was almost impossible to separate them for a moment. However, I did manage to let the rest of them go to Francesca's New Year's Eve party without me. I was rather tired. Apart from having to organize the house party's meals and to cook most of them myself, I had had to rush up to the ranch several times to help Francesca, who was sick. In between I was enjoying our own fiesta enormously, but I thought an evening's rest was a good idea. I had not been writing during the festivities, but I thought writing a chapter would be restful.

I was sorry afterwards that I had missed the New Year's party because someone tried to hit someone over the head with a chair. Archie took off his glasses, a sign that he is contemplating the possibility of intervening in an act of violence, and Hiram rushed into the fray. There was some confusion, and Francesca got tired of everone and went to bed.

That was the only sign of disunity in our Christmas party. Eventually people went away to Mexico City hardly able to tear themselves from the happy atmosphere of Cuernavaca. It was not until months later that we discovered some of the things that had been going on during that Christmas holiday. There was so many emotional entanglements below the surface that they have never been straightened out. I think that Archie and I are the only people of that party who are still on speaking terms with everybody in it.

Archie liked Marjorie. It was so unusual for Archie to like my women friends that I was delighted. It was really Marjory that made Archie seriously consider working on *The Good Neighbour*.

We went up to Mexico City for a while to see how things were shaping up. Marjory had managed to raise some money, enough for Hiram to get an office started. Hiram's idea of an office was to rent an enormous typewriter and several tables. We pointed out that it would be a good idea to get a few chairs. Hiram practically never sat down himself. Marjory explained that when there were any chairs he always leaned on the backs and they broke.

'But still, someone has to use this,' I said, looking at the typewriter.

'That's for Archie,' said Hiram. 'He will be able to get a chair when I'm in the States.'

'Don't worry,' I said. 'He won't need one for the typewriter. He can't type.'

'Good God,' said Hiram. 'I thought everyone could type.'

He was fascinated by the idea that someone could not type. Archie modestly explained that he has always had jobs which provided a typist.

Rafael came in. He groped around looking for a chair. He seemed sick.

'What's the matter with him?' asked Archie.

'He won a hundred pesos in a lottery,' said Hiram. He glanced at me. 'I suppose you'll be pleased about this. Rafael won a hundred pesos and drank it all up.'

'Well, well,' I said.

Rafael could not find a chair, so he sank gently to the ground and propped himself against a wall.

'Now about that dummy—' said Archie.

'Oh, the dummy. Well, I haven't actually got around to doing the dummy yet,' said Hiram.

'My God,' said Archie without heat. 'I suppose you haven't fixed up about an artist either.'

'We haven't a dummy for the artist yet,' said Marjory.

'Quit razzing me,' shouted Hiram. He turned to Archie in triumph. 'And I have got an artist.'

At that moment the door opened slowly. A dirty hand came groping round it. A frayed cuff, a wrinkled sleeve, and a man in a greeny-black suit came shuffling in. He blinked at the party and tears ran out of his eyes. He wiped them away and spoke in a hoarse voice:

'I am here, truly?'

There was a silence. Hiram turned to Archie and seemed slightly perturbed.

'There he is.'

'He is here truly,' said Marjory.

We sent him away because there were no chairs. Hiram explained that the man was an excellent commercial artist.

'After all,' he explained once again. 'Running on a shoe-string like this, we can't expect to get really first-class men. Now if we had more money—'

'You know what,' said Marjory suddenly. 'That's what's the matter with your moustache. You are running it on a shoe-string.'

Marjory and I went away to eat Guymas oysters in the San Juan market. We ate two dozen each and felt fine.

Archie and I discussed the idea of his working on *The Good Neighbour*. It meant a hundred pesos a week and a five day week at that. Twenty dollars a week when we were living on twenty-eight dollars a month was something. Archie could come down on Fridays and go back to Mexico City early Monday morning. I could take over the children, so that we would not lose the five dollars a week for them. It meant that we could save money to make a reserve in case we wanted to move somewhere else. In any case it mean twe could save meony so that we could travel and see Mexico.

Archie asked exactly what he had to do. Hiram explained that he was to take charge of the office. The space-sellers would report to him and he would control their lists; there would be stories to write up about Mexican features; there would be some copywriting for ads. Archie expressed some doubt that there would be much work.

'I shall be away for five weeks,' said Hiram. 'You see how things work out. If you find after a week or two that there isn't enough to warrant a full week, just go up for a day or so and get your pay accordingly. You know, you are a fool not to come in on the project with us.

'I'm satisfied with a salary,' said Archie.

I talked, or rather listened, to Hiram about the Idea. He walked me for miles around Mexico City, explaining, gesticulating, filled with vehement enthusiasm. I began to have faith in Hiram's ability to put it across. The main mystery, why the state departments, foreign consulates, embassies etc. should order it, remained a mystery, but I was so befogged, beaten down under the flood of words, that I felt that Hiram might sell them the Idea. I was utterly worn out with tramping round the back alleys of Mexico City, trotting behind while Hiram strode with his huge feet over torn-up street-car lines, piles of wreckage from demolition gangs, and other things which littered the streets. Hiram particularly loved to stroll around a hospital, built in an icy open square with bitter winds whistling round the guant building. Life in the tropics does not include Mexico City in winter. I really began to feel that if Hiram could get me to walk for miles in high-heeled shoes in mid-winter in Mexico City he could put anything across.

Marjory refused to listen to any more about the Idea. She had raised the money and she felt her part was done.

'You know, I have a feeling that Hiram will pull it off,' I said thoughtfully. We were eating oysters again.

'Sure he will,' she said with her mouth full. 'Hiram is like that. There will be the most terrible crises before it is all over, but it'll work out somehow in the end.'

'I guess I've never appreciated Hiram,' I said. 'I didn't realize he could put such energy into anything.'

'My God!' said Marjory. 'Energy!' Trust Hiram to do everything the hard way. That's why we got divorced. No one could live with Hiram for long.' She thought for a moment. Her neat black brows were drawn together and her dark eyes were full of worry. 'No, I don't think I can manage another dozen. Make it half.' She smiled at me. 'Gee, I love oysters. Ou know, you've made a real hit with Hiram. You don't scare him. He thinks Archie is wonderful, too. Of course, Archie *is* wonderful.'

'Of course he is. Everyone thinks that,' I said. 'Maybe you're right. Half a dozen more is enough. Listen, Marjory, this isn't my business, but whatever did you do to Hiram to make him the way he is?'

Marjory stopped an oyster half-way to her mouth.

'Hell, that wasn't me. It was his first wife who scared the pants off him. She clung. That's why Hiram can't keep still. He's afraid a vine will creep over him if he sits down for a minute. I felt sorry for him. My first husband was a bit of a vine—'

'You Americans amaze me,' I said. 'I feel indecent. Archie and I have been married for nine years. '

Marjory stared at me. Her round black eyes goggled.

'Good God!' she whispered. 'You mean to say you've only been married once to the same man for nine years?'

'Hell,' I said, 'let's have another half dozen each.'

'Sure,' said Marjory. 'For God's sake,' she muttered to herself. 'Nine years. Of course Archie—but nine years. Hey, make mine a dozen,' she said,

Chapter 17
Geese and Irrigation

Marjory had gone back to the States. Archie and I were both sorry when she left. She assured us that she would be back again in less than a year. She was most helpful to me over the American market and wished me luck now that the English market seemed dead. She also wished us both luck with Hiram and *The Good Neighbour*.

Archie had fixed up to go to Mexico City when Hiram left for the States. Hiram was rushing around getting papers fixed and tidying up all the odds and ends ready for Archie to take over. He also promised to have a space-selling staff ready and a typisst by the time he left. Archie went on teaching in Cuernavaca.

We met Colin Bristow casually enough in the Universal Café. He was British, but not unduly so, and he seemed to have roughly the same ideas as we had about the war. It seemed to be obvious that until both sides had exhausted all hope of turning the war against the USSR there would be no real war. The excursion of the USSR against Finland was meat for the red-baiting press and Mannerheim was getting a beautiful build-up as the liberator of the Finnish workers. We had had a liberator in Spain too, with the same Nazi background and backing. It was only by hanging on to past knowledge and refusing to be overwhelmed by the wish-thinkers' outpourings that it was possible to have any idea of what was going on .

Colin Bristow seemed to realize this and we found him pleasant to talk with. He would drop in for a drink under the trees in the evenings, or we would meet him in the

Universal after supper. He and Archie would argue, Archie painstakingly hammering away at point after point while Colin, his red hair falling over his sandy lashes, would bang on the table and scatter the glasses. Sometimes Archie would get bored and leave Colin and me to argue; sometimes we would all three pack into Colin's old green Buick and drive to Tequesquitengo, a charming lake forty kilometres from Cuernavaca, where we could sewim for miles in soft, warm water. Often Archie did not come swimming—even warm water will not tempt him—and Colin and I would drive out there alone. Once we went on from the lake to Taxco, where we had super and drove back along the tortuous mountain road by moonlight. Colin was so overcome by the Mexican night that he nearly drove the Buick straight over one of the twisty corners and there was a slight coldness between us for a while. On the whole, I found Colin pleasant and intelligent and an amusing companion.

A more important event than our acquaintanceship with Colin was the arrival of George and Mary. They moved in at five o'clock in the morning and took a bath in my wash-tub.

George and Mary were two geese, or rather a goose and a gander. I heard a splashing going on outside and got out of bed to see what was happening. I saw a beautiful grey gander sitting in two inches of water trying to wash his neck while a pure white goose looked on with a sneer. That was enough for 5 a.m. and I went back to sleep. When I got up for breakfast the geese were still there. I filled the wash tub and from that moment the geese were there to stay.

Archie and I went out and bought a new and better-shaped tin bath. We sank it into the ground and filled it with clean water. The geese were delighted and spent the morning taking turns swimming. Mary was obviously boss, and every time the old man got comfortably settled down for a nice soak, she would rush off into the woods searching for food. There seemed to be some law that obliged the gander never to allow the goose to be more than three yards away. Mary knew all about this.

When we told Francesca that we had acquired two geese she said it was too much. She had bought a parrot; she had paid for a dog; she had thought that she had acquired six ducks, but the owner turned up and she had to pay for them. The only animals she had for free were five kittens, which she loathed. It seemed that the Johnstone luck was overdoing it with the geese.

Mary obviously wanted to build a nest. She ran hither and thither, closely followed by George, who anxiously examined all the debris that she discarded. Biscuit wanted to play with them, but they pecked his toes. They even chased Capulin, but Capulin managed to retreat in good order. He never actually broke into a run. At last Mary settled on a site. Unfortunately, it was exactly where we had dug a trench to stop the cottage getting flooded when the grounds were irrigated.

After we had been two months in the cottage and the dry season was well under way, the irrigation started. It was very simple. Everyone who had land could have five hours of water pouring over it every fifteen days at a cost of 30 cents. The woods around our cottage were looked after by a *huertero*, who gathered the fruit and saw to the irrigating. He was careful to see that no water spoiled our gravel, and our garden got plenty of water through seepage. We though this irrigating idea was splendid. It kept the woods green and the air fresh. It was all very wonderful until the people on the adjoining land started to water their woods.

Our cottage was built at the bottom of a steep slope.

Behind us, the woods sloped away, a mass of banana trees and coffee bushes, and hidden behind all the foliage was another cottage, bigger than ours. It was some distance away and inhabited by an old lady and her family. Unfortunately the family did not seem to know much about irrigation.

We were sitting in our attractive sitting-room about ten o'clock one night when Archie suddenly started at the floor near our bedroom dooor. I thought he must have found an outsize in scorpions. But it was just a little trickle of water. We though the cistern must be leaking. We examined the cistern. Then we decided that it must be the outside tank. The tank was all right. Then I felt my feet squeeze into the ground. I saw that from behind the house, little shining rivulets were pouring rapidly past the bathroom window into our garden.

We managed to sidetrack the water to some extent, but the house was filled. It poured straight through and out at the end of the sitting-room.

I rushed over to the neighbour's house, but the old lady was helpless. She said that it was a surprise to her, all her drying coffee beans had been spoiled. She supposed that someone must have asked for water, but she really did not know. In any case, no one ever knew just when it was one's turn. It seemed a calamity all round.

There were advantages in having a porous house. We slept with our beds scarcely touching the floor; by the morning the place was damp but the water was still pouring down the steps from the house. We decided to dig a trench.

The old lady was perfectly agreeable. She did not mind how many trenches we dug in her land. Unfortunately, we discovered that a trench was useless, because most of the water found an underground runway and bubbled up in the middle of the bathroom floor. We began to wonder if we should move.

We had both become attached to the cottage. The one good room, the sitting-room, was perfectly proportioned, so that one always felt comfortable in it. The garden was growing and we practically lived out under the big trees. Small houses were hard to find. The little prim houses on the wrong side of the *barranca* did not attact us.

Mary settled things by suddenly laying five eggs with great rapidity in a heap of leaves in the irrigation ditch. George became violently ferocious. He would rush madly at anyone who went near the nest, making horrible noises and looking murderous. It was a fine performance so long as the enemy reacted properly. I had to do the washing and George just had to put up with me passing and repassing the nest. He never failed to rush, but after a while he learned to turn aside when I did not run away and to become intensely engrossed in something near by. He would choose a small plant and give it hell.

I tried moving the eggs to a safer spot. Mary looked surprised, but went right on sitting in the heap of leaves. In the end I gave up. Mary got her eggs back and we hoped for the best.

Obviously we could not move until Mary's family was hatched. Something went wrong with the next two weeks' watering and the old lady did not get any. I think my friend, Don Faustino, sabotaged her.

Don Faustino was an old man living in a tiny adobe house deep in the woods. I used to meet him in the woods and we became friends. I thought the geese might be from his small farm, but he assured me that they were not. He told me to keep them, they must have come a long distance looking for water. Maria, our neighbours' maid, said most likely Don Faustino had brought them himself; it was his way of giving me a present. I did not think that this was likely.

He was horrified when he heard about the water and promised he would do what he could. His house was near one of the places where the streams were switched in various directions. The irrigation method was simple. The water was carried from the hills along the ridges between the deep cuts that divide Cuernavaca longitudinally and it was allowed to escape down the sides when anyone needed it. Don Faustino was a lonely old man. He asked me if I thought that Maria would like to marry him. Perhaps I would find out. I told Maria, who said, '*Ay, madre mía,*' several times and then said, 'No.' I told Don Faustino no. He sighed and said that he had thought not.

Mary sat on her eggs peacefully except for twice a day, when she moved off for food and exercise. This was a trying time for George. He was having a wonderful sense of freedom with Mary tied to her nest, although she called him back if he strayed too far. But when she left the nest George did not know what to do. She stretched herself, spread her wings, and ran shrieking through the trees. George tried to follow her and to stay by the eggs at the same time. It was difficult, and he usually stuck half-way, screaming in his high-pitched treble. Mary, still yelling, came tearing back like an express train and snatched a mouthful or two of food. Then she went back to the nest and carefully counted the eggs. Then she sat down with much plumping out of feathers and there was complete silence.

Another reason for not moving was that Archie had to go up to Mexico City. Hiram came down in a great state to say that he was leaving at once for the States with Rafael. Everything was settled. There was money for Archie's salary for five weeks; money for Hiram and Rafael for five weeks. The Good Neighbours was an actual fact. All Archie had to do was to go to Mexico and carry on until Hiram came back with dozens of circulation orders and advertising contracts from the States.

I did not mind being alone for five days in the week. I would always rather be with Archie, but I never get bored by myself. I did the housework and worked in the mornings; I had lunch and rested the early part of the afternoon. Then I worked for a couple of hours until it was tiome to take Biscuit out for a run. Sometimes Colin would come to take me up to the Universal for a drink, but usually I worked after an early supper and then went to bed early. I needed plenty of sleep.

Archie came down on Fridays and went back Monday mornings. He seemed to be alternately furious, miserable, and bored to tears. It seemed that Hiram had rushed off leaving hundreds of ends untied; a number of interviews which meant endless hanging around people's officers; no proper organization for space-selling; in fact, Archie was left holding the bag. The only consolation was that his pay was all arranged so that there was no trouble about that. Archie had told Hiram that if there was a hitch about his pay he would drop the whole concern.

Hiram wrote no letters. He and Rafael just gently dropped out of existence. Archie grimly went up to Mexico and worked until late each night so that he could get down on Fridays. He lived for his weekends.

The unfortunate part about Archie finding himself left with the full responsibility for something about whose inner working he knew practically nothing was that he could not bring himself to believe that *The Good Neighbour* would ever come out. There is nothing so pessimistic as a Scot. The Irish tend to the other extreme, and I believed that *The Good Neighbour* would materialize. Archie and I would argue about it, with Colin listening in. Colin was a serious writer, one who writes because he has to get it out of his system, and he was gently scornful of our commercialized minds. He could not imagine why anyone should get excited about a publication which was nothing but a vehicle for advertising.

'This Hiram sounds impossibly interested in money,' said Colin. 'He must be a dull chap.'

'Hiram isn't dull,' I said. 'He is a bit wild—'

'Huh,' snorted Archie. 'He is criminally wild.'

'What are his politics?' asked Colin.

'Oh, Hiram hasn't any politics,' I said. 'At least nothing important. He sometimes thinks he would like to be a Communist, but he doesn't know anything about it.'

Colin frowned. 'I suppose you know that I used to be a member of the Party at one time,' he said in an odd voice.

'Why did they kick you out?' I asked. I was not very interested. Colin was one of those charming intellectuals who would never be any use under real discipline.

Colin flushed. 'I was not kicked out,' he said. 'I left because I could not see eye to eye with the Party on one particular issue.

'Yes?' I said. 'By the way, where was this? In England or the States?'

'That,' said Colin firmly, 'is neither here nor there.'

'Just like Hiram,' said Archie bitterly. 'My God, when I get hold of that—'

'I just thought I'd mention it,' said Colin. 'You'd be bound to find out.'

'What does it matter?' I said. 'We've managed to have some good arguments. After all, I'm not a member of any Communist Party, so what?'

Colin looked at me and I was struck by something peculiar in his expression.

'Just what is the trouble with you?' I asked.

'How could he have any troubles?' said Archie. 'I've got them all. I am the one who has to go up to Mexico to deal with the halt, maimed and blind. Have you ever seen our space-sellers?'

Chapter 18
Chorus of Space-Sellers

I had not seen Archie's space-sellers. Hiram had gathered them together at the last moment because he had seen something in Archie's eye when he suggested leaving Archie to find them for himself. As Hiram said afterwards, it is not possible to get the best on a shoe-string. Also he was pressed for time. When I did seen them I was surprised that he had managed to collect three such specimens in a short space of time. Looking at them, one would think they had to be collected on at a time over a large area.

I saw them when I paid Archie a visit in Mexico. We were talking together in the office, now provided with chairs, wh7en there was a scratching sound at the door. It opened slowly and three men came in. They crawled, hopped, and sprang into the room.

The first man was a salesman who had once been called dynamic. He burst into the room and struck an attitude. He had a full chest and bulging thighs and his suit was too tight. He had a flashing smile and a wandering eye.

'Well, well, well,' he boomed and the air was filled with a mixture of garlic and aniseed.

The second man was tiny. He had abnormally long arms, which gave the impression that he shuffled along the ground by their aid. He had a shrill voice and obviously suffered from various obscure diseases.

The third man hopped into the room and sank into a chair. He had a dead white face and a hare lip. He suffered from corns.

'Any news?' asked Archie.

A strange hoarse cry answered him which he interpreted from long practice to mean 'no', uttered by all three.

'Haven't they sold any space yet?' I asked. Somehow one did not think of addressing them directly. But they answered together like a vaudeville team.

'Three pages.'

'Archie, that's wonderful. Three pages.'

Archie looked apologetic. 'It's really only one page,' he explained. 'They each brought back the same page.'

They took up positions around the man sitting in the chair. They waited expectantly. I felt that I should have a bag of something, to throw them morsels. I could not decide whether I should throw peanuts or raw meat.

'Archie, what are they waiting for?' I asked.

'They always wait for money,' said Archie simply.

'But they don't get paid on commission?'

'Yes, you know that and I know that but it seems that Hiram said something about a weekly salary.'

'Did he leave any money for a weekly salary?'

'Oh, no,' said Archie.

'Haven't you told them that?'

'Oh, yes,' said Archie.

'Oh,' I said.

There was no news from Hiram. Archie had written dozens of letters, mostly imploring explanations of half-finished items which baffled him. The letters varied from bitter irony to infuriated threats but Hiram ignored them all. The States had swallowed Hiram and Rafael completely.

At the end of five weeks Archie was ready to quit. He had done all that was possible. Getting ads for an unknown quantity with a group of monstrosities for salesmen was impossible. Anyhow, selling space was not Archie's business. When the hearty young man with breath like a cloud disappeared for three weeks, Archie made an effort to trace him and then conscientiously left messages pinned to the table every time he left the office. He wrote all the messages on large sheets of paper and each day he removed the sheet from the table to a hook on the wall. By the end of three weeks there was quite a dossier. But the hearty young man was in Toluca and sent a cable asking for money to get home. Archie wrote him an answer on another piece of paper and pinned it to the table.

I still had faith in Hiram. Archie, doubtful from the beginning of the idea, now was convinced that Hiram had seen the impracticability of the scheme and had no intention of returning to Mexico. That did not seem like my interpretation of Hiram's character but everyone we knew agreed with Archie. There was enough money for three weeks' salary left and Archie decided to carry on until the money was used. Then he would wind up the whole show and quit.

We had news of Rafael. I was unfortunately back in Cuernavaca when Conchita burst in on Archie.

She was fat with oily black curls and fists the size of hams. She screamed that she wanted her money.

Archie was tired of people wanting money. He told her to go away.

She said that Rafael had promised her money. He had promised to send her money every week. She had not received a penny. She was Rafael's wife. She was entitled to her money. It must be that Archie was stealing it all.

Archie says he was dignified and controlled throughout the interview. I would love to have been there.

Conchita finally seemed to be persuaded that Archie was

not embezzling. Then she decided that Archie was most *simpático*. She wept a little and cleared her throat and spat out of the window.

'I have no one, no one at all,' she moaned. 'Rafael had his faults, but after all he was someone.'

Archie said nervously that surely Rafael would turn up again.

'Did the *señor* not know?' asked Conchita in surprise. 'How strange that the *señor* has not heard. Rafael is in trouble. There was something about a cheque. He was thirsty.'

Archie came down to Cuernavaca and told me that he was through. He would go back at his own expense just to tidy up all the ends. He intended to write to everyone to say that The Good Neighbour was not coming out. I persuaded him not to do this. I agreed that he should come home and close the office, but the rent was paid for another two months and, as far as we knew, Hiram was not in jail. I still had faith in Hiram.

Shortly after Archie's return our geese were due to hatch their eggs. Mary had been sitting for twenty-seven days. Don Faustino had worked wonders of sabotage with the irrigation. On the twenty-seventh night he failed us. We woke up to find our beds practically floating. The garden was flooded. The eggs were washed away and the geese were preparing to leave.

There was nothing to be done about the eggs. We shut the geese in the woodshed and went back to bed. I felt almost as frustrated as if I had say for twenty-seven days on five eggs. It was obvious that the geese did not wish to stay in such a place. We took them up to Francesca's *rancho* and gave them to her.

On top of the egg tragedy, we heard that our cottage had

been sold. We would have to move out in a month.

We were sad in some ways, but at least this made up our minds for us. The water, the drinking water, had been getting steadily scarcer; living under the trees during the rainy season would be unpleasant; the bi-weekly flooding was overdoing discomfort. We rushed down to the wrong side of the *barranca* to see if any of the houses were still to rent.

There was one. We looked it over carefully. There was no doubt that it was a villa, with shining tiled floors and high ceilings. When we had first seen the houses I had disliked the modernness of them. Now they seemed highly desirable residences. The house we saw had a big terrace high above the road, two large rooms opening off it; a tiled bathroom with a sunk bath and shower; a large covered back porch with the kitchen opening off it. One of the rooms had a door on to both front and back porches. There was a patch of garden around the house, but it and eight similar houses of various designs were built in a large *quinta*, or garden. The rent was nine dollars a month.

We were determined that there must be a snag. Water! We saw the greenness of the lawns around the houses and noticed the water jets playing over them. There certainly seemed to be plenty of water. The windows had screening, there were built-in closets, the houses were in good repair. We puzzled for some time. Then I remembered Mrs Hartley had been perfectly serious when she said one could not live on the wrong side of the *barranca*.

The foreigners resident in Mexico seem to think that it is impossible to know any Mexicans. They may count a few rich Mexican families among their acquaintances but they would not consider being on friendly terms with middle class Mexicans. It would not occur to them. The wrong side of the *barranca* was the wrong side because only Indians and Mexicans lived there.

I suited us perfectly. We did not wish to know foreigners, we wanted to know Mexicans. To make it all more interesting, our front terrace overlooked the *barranca*, the near side of which was covered with *jacales*, little shacks where the poorer Indians lived. We could get an idea of how not so rich Mexicans and really poor Mexicans lived by sitting on our front porch or our back porch.

I have never quite understood when a Mexican is not a Mexican. Technically the term must apply to all people who are citizens of Mexico, but Indians will explain with great pride that they are pure Indian and certain Mexicans will take pains to point out that they are entirely 'white'. Others consider themselves Spaniards, but this is getting a little awkward with the influx of Spanish refugees. The Mexican Spaniards have little in common with the Spaniards of Republican Spain. Most Mexicans have some Indian blood and many of the Indians who say they are *puro indio* have some Spanish blood, while the Mexican Spaniards are not entirely free from a hint of Indian blood occasionally. The Indians are undoubtedly the purest races in Mexico while the *mestizo*, or mixed race, is the most common in the official classes.

We decided to rent the house and arranged with the man acting for the owner that we would move in in a few weeks. In the meantime I had a birthday.

There was nothing important about the birthday except that I realized that I was having a birthday in Mexico. In 1939 I had my birthday in the South of France, shortly after leaving Spain. In 1938 Archie and I were paying a short visit to England during the Spanish war and I had my birthday in London. In 1937 I had my birthday in

Barcelona in an air-raid. In 1936 I had my birthday celebrations in Marcus' bar in Tossa, Catalunya, with the assistance of our hotel guests. This time, 1940, I had a birthday party in Mexico under the tropical night sky and I wondered where I might have the next one.

Archie and I fully realized our luck in getting to Mexico. Out of all the people who declared they would miss the next war by going to Mexico, we were the only ones who actually got there. Francesca and João shared our luck, literally shared it because without us they would never have made the trip. Everyone else had put it off until it was too late, or were unable to raise the money or simply let things drift. We wished we had been firmer with Leon about coming out but he had to live his own life. Later we heard that he was in a concentration camp in Britain. Still later we heard that it would have been a waste of time to be firm with him. He had become engaged to an English girl, which accounted in great measure for his reluctance to come to Mexico.

We sat under the stars and regretted leaving the cottage. In the dry weather it could have been perfect except for the lack of water in the cisterns and the redundance of water in the house. The weather was sublime. I had never believed there could be such a climate. Day after day of brilliant sunshine, never too hot, and even in the evenings seldom too cold. I did not wear trousers, as I had done in Spain. Trousers seemed out of place in a big town. Cuernavaca was the capital of the state of Morelos and not a little fishing village. I wore instead blouses and skirts made out of the Indian cottons, which most Indians use only for aprons. The Indian idea of richness is to have a crimson satin frock. They thought I was crazy to wear their apron material for skirts when I must be able to afford the cheap satin. My skirts, of all colours and patterns, cost about 25 cents each, and I had about a dozen, which I usually wore with white, short-sleeved blouses. Archie wore pants made of a woven cotton which looked like linen, and sports shirts to match. A suit of shirt and long pants cost about two dollars, including the making of the pants. I made the shirts and my own clothes with the aid of Francesca's sewing-machine.

Francesca was making a little money out of dressmaking. She had been a professional dressmaker at one time and people were delighted to find someone who could fit properly. She was in difficulties with getting money out of England and the idea of running her *rancho* as a guest house was not so good. Francesca was a wonderful cook and, like so many people who adore cooking, she could not bear to be economical. Her guests must have the very best, and while the guests grew fat Francesca found that she was running out of money. With the worry about money, she began to think she did not like Mexico. She was restless and every time I saw her she had another wonderful idea about some perfectly marvellous country where one needed no visas or papers and where the exchange was so in one's favour that living was too cheap for words. At first I took everything seriously and wasted a lot of thought and trouble to prove that there was no such place in the world, but then I found out that it was just a passing craze and that next time it would be some other idea. Even her dislike of Mexico varied according to the state of her health and the latest news about getting money out of England.

I suddenly realized, through Francesca, that I no longer disliked Mexico. I had never discussed my dislike with anyone and I found it was not there any more. I had accepted Mexico completely, almost unconsciously. I could not understand when visitors complained about the dirt in the streets; I was no longer aware of the armless, legless beggars; I took it for granted that officials could be corrupt. My acceptance of conditions was perhaps carried too far on occasion. A friend complained that she could never buy again at a certain store which sold milk because she saw the storekeeper fishing flies out of the milk with his finger.

'But after all,' I protested, 'he *was* trying to remove the flies.'

Flies, scorpions, spiders, all seemed very small in Mexico. At last I could realize what a vast, undeveloped country it was and its infinite possibilities. In Europe I had the feeling that everything was over, at least for many years, and that those years until a new order could be established would be thick with bombs and blood. In Mexico there seemed to be a feeling of youth. In spite of the ancient Indian culture that hung over the land, the country was young, according to our ideas of civilization. One sensed the youngness. One also sensed that the Mexicans were aware. They had learned something from years of fighting and oppression. The Mexicans might not be able to do much about the strong hand of the United States, but they knew all about it. After the Hear, See, Think No Evil policy of Europe during the last few years, it was a relief to be in a country where people did not clap their hands over their monkey ears, eyes and mouths.

Chapter 19
Soul of a Bank

Shortly before Archie packed up *The Good Neighbour* we arranged our Mexican papers. The Mexican Government was kind enough to treat us as refugees, and they granted us temporary papers. In order to make everything easier all round, we had a friend in New York transfer a sum of money to enable us to open an account in a New York bank. With all the difficulties of transferring money from England, I was not sure how much of my outside earnings we could count upon and the Mexican Government would never believe that two foreigners could live on the small sums we earned in Mexico.

We knew nothing about American banks. Our only knowledge of banks was based on the old-world, fatherly atmosphere of London banks. Our London bank manager was a charming man who willingly did a hundred and one small favours for us, and in return we kept him posted on our adventures, which he declared opened windows in his soul. Our American friends told us that American bank managers either have no souls or the windows are tightly jammed.

We gave no thought to American bank managers' souls. We merely deposited one thousand three hundred dollars and asked that an account be opened. In due course we received a cheque book.

Archie was still up in Mexico when a little man with a shiny derby hat came to the cottage. He wanted to see Archie. He said is was really the *señor* he had come to see but perhaps I would be interested in this. He handed me a printed paper headed Dun & Bradstreet which seemed to be about something to do with importing or exporting. I had never heard of the people and I was not interested in importing or exporting. I thanked the unpleasant little man and gave him back the paper.

'I am sure you will be interested to register with us,' he said with an oily smile. 'Just fill up the enclosed form and any time you want information to help your business, just ask us.'

I explained shortly that we had no business. He persisted. I grew annoyed and told him to go away. He kept thrusting the forms at me as he backed towards the gate. He looked at the cottage and asked me if I owned it. He wanted to know what rent we paid. I was furious.

'Get the hell out of here,' I said, but unfortunately it sounds more polite in Spanish. He tipped his shiny derby and scuttled up the road.

I had forgotten the incident, but I visited Archie and he told me a story. It seemed that a little man with a shiny hat had come to see him. The little man had asked many impertinent questions and had tried to get Archie to fill in a form with all details about his "business". In the end Archie had threatened to throw him down the stairs. He had tipped his hat and scuttled away.

Archie is far more astute in these things than I am. He had immediately had an idea and he rang up the firm whose illustrious name was on the form. Archie had never heard of them. He explained that he had just removed one of their representatives. He asked what the devil they meant by sending little men in derby hats to worry him. The voice at the other end of the wire was apologetic. It was all a mistake. Archie asked why they wanted to make inquiries about him. Had someone asked the firm to do so?

After some hesitation the voice admitted that this was so. Archie had an illuminating thought. Was it the New York bank? It was.

I sat down and wrote a letter to the bank.

> Dear Sirs,
>
> My husband and I have been pestered by some odd little men in Derby hats pretending to be anxious to help us with our business. We have found it quite impossible to convince them that we have no business. Eventually we became exasperated by the continual infringement of our privacy and liberties and we were rather firm with them. We then discovered that they were employed by your bank as sleuths.
>
> We understand that all countries have their own methods. Of course we are used only to the rather old-fashioned courtesy of London banks [I gave the name of our bank] and we are not complaining at your methods in dealing with would-be clients. But we do think we are entitled to ask you to employ better sleuths. We don't mind a bit being shadowed or even having our correspondence opened, but we would rather have it done neatly. We do object to amateurish little men in Derby hats haunting our doorsteps and asking us what seem irrelevant and impertinent questions.
>
> I am afraid your sleuths don't like us any more. But of course we did not know they were your sleuths. Would it perhaps be simpler if we gave you some references and information generally?
>
> [Follows a list of references in London and the United States].
>
> Please do not think we are complaining about your business methods. We have heard about American banks before and presume you find such methods necessary. But we really do object strongly to having

our time wasted by such incompetent people as Dun & Bradstreet seem to employ. They would make excellent bailiffs but as detectives they are hopeless. It took my husband over half an hour to make one of them state his business and go away. (He went). We are busy people and haven't time to convince Dun & Bradstreet that we have no business in Mexico, have never had a business in Mexico, and do not intend to start a business in Mexico.

We need a statement from you that we have 1,300 dollars in our account. This is necessary for us as English residents in Mexico. I also have travellers cheques here for 100 dollars which I would like to send, but perhaps after hearing the sad report from your sleuths you do not want our account. If you agree to take our account, I want that statement and I want it quickly.

Yours faithfully, etc.

The New York bank was amused and horror-stricken. Since then we have closed our account because our friend wanted his thousand dollars back, but the bank continues to act as unofficial agent for our affairs. It forwards letters, sends on cables, and puts us in touch with people in the States who lose our address. If we ever have another thousand dollars to spare we will certainly open a real account and in the meantime we hotly deny the contention of most Americans that American banks are snooty.

We were packed up ready to move into our new home when Archie returned from a visit to the man in charge of the *quinta* to say that we could not have the house after all.

We had arranged with the owner's son, who was acting as his father's agent. That the inside of the house should be whitewashed. The walls were a strange shade of robin's egg blue and my furniture was mostly yellow. The blue was coming off in patches and the man agreed to have a coat of whitewash put over it. Archie went down to see if the whitewashing had been done and each time he was told that the men were coming in the very next day. The day before we were supposed to move in, the whitewashing still was not done. I decided that we should call it a day and do without the whitewashing.

But then Archie came back with the bad news. It had been rented to some people from Mexico City. Archie tried to see the owner's son but he was in Mexico City. So we were faced with a problem.

The greatest problem was that small houses were difficult to find in Cuernavaca. There were any amount of big villas with three or four bedrooms and swimming pool renting from forty dollars a month, but two-room cottages were rare. We spent the morning of the next day in a frantic drive around the town with a house agent and we saw some horrible dark apartments at fifteen to twenty dollars but nothing comparable with the houses on the wrong side of the *barranca*. In the end I said we would just move in and defy them to turn us out. I was not very sure of myself in Mexico. In Spain there would have been no question of not getting the house. We were experts at turning even chiefs of police out of their houses, but Mexico was incalculable. It was quite a possibility that one could be turned out of a house in Mexico: the owner would probably burn it over one's head without a qualm.

However, we were packed up and due to leave the cottage, so we decided to take a chance on it. I slipped down that evening and locked all the doors of the house and took away the keys. That meant that no one else could get in. The following morning Archie and I went down to view the situation before bringing our furniture in a truck. We found the superintendent wringing his hands. Someone had stolen the keys.

I explained that I had the keys. I explained that we were moving in, in half an hour. He denied this. He declared the house was rented. We agreed. It was rented, to us. He almost wept. He could do nothing but obey orders from the owners. We asked him if the son of the owner was back from Mexico City. He was still absent. We said we were sorry, but we were moving in, right then.

The superintendent was a little man with a mean little face and shifty eyes. He tried a last shot.

'*Señores*, the house isn't' whitewashed.'

'So what?' I said. 'I don't care about the whitewashing. I would rather sleep with that blue than in the street. I tell you we have already left our other house. We are going to move into this one.'

His face brightened. 'You mean that you would be willing to take the house without the whitewashing?' he said in unbelieving tones.

'Naturally. Whitewashing is not important. What is important is—'

'But, *señores*, in that case—why, of course, then the house is yours.'

Archie and I gaped at him. 'But you said it was rented—'

'Oh, that,' he smiled deprecatingly and plucked some dead flowers off a bush. 'Well, in a manner of speaking it is rented, of course, but that can easily be arranged. If you are willing to take it without the whitewashing, then everything is different. I shall be delighted to allow you to enter immediately.'

I was careful not to smile at his magnanimous gestures. I

had the keys.

We had a hilarious move. Archie persuaded some friendly people from a *pulquería* around the corner to move everything in their truck. He explained that it was a small amount of furniture. They sent a bright yellow truck with the name of the cantina on it—El Templo de Amor. They also sent eight men. Our furniture was whisked out of the house and the place was practically sacked. Old bottles, piles of junk, torn papers waiting for the garbage man vanished into the pockets of the light-fingered attendants of the temple of love. Someone found an old tin of cyan gas which we used to destroy the red harvest ants. He sniffed at it appreciatively and asked if he might take it with him. He thought it would add flavour to the *pulque*.

The truck, with my garden transferred to earthenware pots as ballast, went straight down a hill I had always considered as impassable to motorists and arrived at the house with only one pot broken. The eight men tossed up our battered furniture in a few minutes and gathered round for drinks. We felt we could not do them justice with a few sips of rum after their own *pulque* but they were very polite and seemed happy. They were somewhat restless and we found out that they were longing to get back to the empty house in case there was some loot. We had locked the house, which contained some few pieces of furniture which belonged there, but we told the men that anything thrown away or left in the outhouses was theirs. Later we heard that the house had been broken open and everything taken out and we felt that our friends had let us down. However, the house was broken into three time more during the following six months, the new owners having decided not to take possession after all, so we have give our friends of the *pulquería* the benefit of the doubt.

The first few weeks were spent in trying to get some colours somewhere that went with other colours. The blue was difficult, but a brilliant pink dado and various coloured tiles were baffling. In the end I decided to paint all the woodwork, including our furniture, a deep cream, eliminate the pink, and do the chairs over in Mexican style with a soft tomato red. I was discouraged in my efforts to do anything about the house because I was just learning what it was like to live with noise. I was certain that I could never get used to radios, children screaming in the street, a blacksmith across the road, and a carpenter next door to him. I have been told that our *quinta* is extremely quiet compared to most places not buried in a jungle, but it seemed bedlam to me. Archie watched me anxiously, expecting me to get up one morning and say casually that we were removing to Chile, but I managed to stick it out. Other problems arose which made a little noise seem the most natural thing in the world.

I had noticed that for some weeks Colin Bristow had been behaving oddly. He shied like a frightened horse if I asked him for a lift in his car. He nearly passed away when I suggested he take me into Mexico City for a day's shopping. I wondered vaguely if he could possibly be so foolish as to think I had designs on him matrimonially or otherwise. But it seemed too absurd when everyone knew how oddly attached Archie and I were to each other. There was no doubt that there was something the matter with Colin and there arose a chain of circumstances that seemed to be always bringing us together. There was the day Colin had his car in the garage and went to Mexico City by bus and I was in the seat behind him. Archie and I went together to the movies, which we did rarely, and Colin was sitting behind us. I went to swim in a nearby lake with some friends and chose a day when Colin drove over with some friends. It did not strike me as peculiar because one was always running into people in a small place, but Colin seemed agitated every time we came across one another. He still came down to visit us from time to time but appeared ill at ease. I could not imagine what was the matter with him, but I did not give it much thought. Francesca asked me why he had asked her innumerable questions about me but I had no idea.

'He particularly wanted to know if you were a Communist,' she said.

'What did you tell him?' I asked.

'Oh, I told him I didn't know. I don't think I would know if anyone was a Communist. He seemed to think you were *very* left.'

'It is a pity that people use labels so much,' I said. 'Anyone who has liberal ideas must be a Communist and anyone with reactionary ideas must be a Fascist. Actually it isn't so at all. At the most one can say a liberally-minded person is more likely to support the Communist Party than a reactionary, and a reactionary is a potential Fascist.'

'Colin seems very nervous these days,' remarked Francesca, sewing rapidly as usual. Francesca was always doing something rapidly.

'He positively jitters,' I said happily.

'Mrs Halliday is worried about him. Oh, yes, and she told Colin she thought you were a Communist.'

'Now, who is Mrs Halliday?' I asked patiently.

Mrs Halliday was a gay old lady with the tattered remnants of good looks to which she clung with the tenacity of a Boston bull. I had seen her around and wondered why, but I had never spoken to her or of her and I had no idea of her name. It appeared that she was a sort of flypaper for rumours—she hung herself up in the middle of Cuernavaca and the poor little rumours kicked and struggled and buzzed helplessly for a while and finally fell off exhausted to cling stickily to whatever might be passing.

I left Francesca with two new cooking recipes and a blouse she had made for me, a pot of marmalade and some pickles. Colin's idiosyncrasies and Mrs Halliday's peculiarities had slipped my mind. Archie and I had had a trying day in Mexico. Francesca had come up with us and somehow we all three gone up in different buses at different times. We managed to foregather to come back together and we had supper at the *rancho*. Francesca was sick and I was worried about her. I also had a novel to finish for my English publishers, who were braving the war and wanted something light and outside the war area. I had plenty to think about. The next morning we glanced at the papers and saw that an attempt had been made on Leon Trotsky in his house in Coyoacán, just outside Mexico City. The right press was howling that it was done by the Communists, the lone left paper was bleating that it was a plot to discredit the Communists. We just noted the fact that several men with a machine gun had apparently missed hitting the old man and we wondered why. Archie said:

'I'm a swell newspaper man. You realize that happened yesterday when we were in Mexico. Now I should have smelled that it was going to happen and stayed up for it.'

'If you had, there wouldn't have been an attempt,' I said, eating Francesca's marmalade. 'You know how everything stops when you are around.'

Chapter 20
Nest of International Spies

The Trotsky attempt was a topic of conversation for a few days. Then more important events put it out of my mind. Francesca became really sick and I went to stay up at the *rancho* in order to look after her guests so that she could stay in bed.

Archie stayed in our new house to look after Biscuit, but came up to the *rancho* for his meals. I had been installed in Francesca's house one day when a kindly visitor came to see her. It was Mrs Halliday. I was in the kitchen when she arrived so I missed yet another chance of meeting Mrs Halliday. I bore up bravely.

When she had left, Francesca told me that Mrs Halliday was so upset to hear that Archie and I were getting a divorce. Such a devoted couple, we had always seemed to be. But one simply never knew, did one? Francesca was furious. She was the most loyal soul in the world and she was not amused when I laughed about it. I said I did not care what the old Vultures and Harpies of Cuernavaca hatched about me.

That evening I went down to the Universal to meet Archie after supper. He was sitting there waiting for me with Colin. Colin rose nervously when I arrived and dashed away. Archie remarked that the man's nerves seemed all shot to pieces. We stayed and talked for a bit and Archie walked part of the way back to the *rancho*. He returned to the Universal to find Biscuit, who had stayed behind, visiting some dog friends in the neighbourhood, and Colin joined him again. After a few minutes a friend of Colin's, a pretty blonde girl, joined them. Presently Archie went home with Biscuit.

The next day, after one of Francesca's lunches, we were all idling on the terrace of the *rancho*. Francesca's guests were reading books; I was helping Francesca with some sewing; Archie was making copious notes for a book which he admits he is never going to write. Suddenly the door leading from the house on to the terrace burst open and we were surrounded by fifteen armed men.

It was quite surprising. One minute we were so peaceful and the next, tough looking Mexicans with revolvers were pushing around, looking under cushions, brushing us aside, shaking books open, snatching the sewing out of my hands. I uprose and demanded explanations of one of the men.

'What on earth are you doing here?' I asked. 'Who are you and what do you want?'

He shrugged and waved his pistol. I gathered that it had nothing to do with him. I approached another man who looked like someone in authority.

'Hey, what is all this?' I asked.

I had taken charge because I speak fairly good Spanish and also I had a good conditioning on pistols in the early days of the Spanish war. I was used to anarchists with pistols and consequently always expect everyone to behave with the same easy charm. Archie is equally nonchalant about firearms, but he is slow to get his meaning across. So I tackled the chief of the *pistoleros*. To my surprise he said shortly:

'I want the Señora Johnstone.'

'Well, here she is,' I said. 'Now perhaps you will explain just why you have broken in here.'

He condescended to show me his police card. It

appeared he was the head of the Mexican secret police. I was impressed.

'Well, what do you want me for?' I asked.

The chief called together his band and told them to keep an eye on the others. He took me into Francesca's bedroom to be questioned. Archie was sent into another bedroom. The rest of the people were left on the porch.

The chief eyed me across the table. He was a pleasant-looking little man with shrewd eyes.

'Where were you before you came to Mexico?' he asked.

'In France,' I answered.

'Aha!' he said. 'In prison.'

He used the word *preso*, where I was used to the Spanish word *carcel* so I did not understand him.

'Where was I?' I asked.

'In prison. In a French prison,' said the chief impatiently. 'In prison for being a Communist.'

'Nonsense,' I said.

'Where were you before that?'

'Before I was in France, not in prison, and not a Communist,' I said, 'I was in Spain.' I knew that might cause trouble but he could easily check up by my passport.

'Oh, in a Spanish prison! For being a Nazi!'

'Make up your mind,' I said.

He stared at me. He was impressed by the fact that I was not in the least afraid of him. I had perfect confidence in my record. I was nervous because I had overheard one of the *pistoleros* mention something about taking us all to Mexico City. He mentioned taking Archie in particular. I did not want to go to Mexico City and I certainly did not want Archie and me to be separated. However, the chief did not realize that I was at all nervous.

'Well, just what are your politics?' he asked.

'I am a writer,' I said grandiloquently. 'I make myself plain in my books. Why don't you read them?'

This shook him. It was a ghastly thought. He became more pleasant.

'You may be able to help me,' he said. 'Tell me everything you know about all the people in this house.'

'Francesca is my dearest friend,' I said. 'She is sick. I don't know anything at all about the other people.'

He shot a question at me. 'What are you doing living apart from your husband?'

'I'm not.'

'Ha! Yes you are. You are living here and he is living elsewhere.'

'I'm staying here to help my friend who is sick.'

He leered at me. 'I suppose you know that your husband is having an affair with a blonde.'

'Oh really? How do you know?'

'We watch. We have been watching for some time. Last night when you left the Universal, a blonde joined your husband and he went home with her.'

'Sure, a blond dog,' I said, thinking of Biscuit.

'The dog was there too. He went back pretending to fetch the dog but it was the blonde he was after.'

'You are sure about this?' I asked.

'Positively.'

'Then why on earth ask me why I'm not living with the man?'

We got on very well after that. When I could escape, he asked me to send in Francesca. Francesca marched in as if she were going to the day of judgement.

I was anxious about Archie. He seemed to be shut up in the other bedroom. One of the *pistoleros* told me he was *incomunicado*. I ran round the outside and peered in through the screening. Archie was sitting in a chair with his feet up on the table. He was reading a detective story.

'Hist!' I said dramatically.

'Oh, hello,' said Archie. 'I'd like a drink.'

'How can I get it through the screening?'

Archie looked surprised. 'Must you get it through the screening? Why not bring it through the door?'

We had a quite a party. Some of the *pistoleros* came in. They had some statements from the other guests that they wanted me to translate and type out. I said I would do it as a favour, but we were thirsty. There was a noise of cars starting up and three cars drove off to return shortly with two bottles of rum. The police gave them to us with a flourish. I said I would work for them after that.

Before I could get going there was a noise of rifle fire. The *pistoleros* dashed away and there was some confusion around the house. We could see some of the Cuernavaca mounted police seemed to be involved. Presently all was quiet and the *pistoleros* came back again. There had been a little *equivocació*n. One of the women living in some huts outside the *rancho* grounds had thought we were being held up by bandits and had sent down to fetch up the Cuernavaca police. They gallantly came galloping to rescue us from the Mexico City secret police.

After this we settled down to serious business. Francesca's guests were pleasant people, but difficult in such a situation. One was French, Joao was Portuguese, another guest was a Finn. The Frenchman was a radio fan and had two radios and innumerable spare parts. It was confusing for the police.

We could not discover what the police were looking for. They had my name, the only name they knew in the party. They thought it was my radio. They refused to say what they were after.

We all made statements. Archie and I, veterans of Spanish police raids, were shocked at the brusqueness of the Mexican police. We realized that we had been spoiled in Spain and were prepared to accept Mexican methods. We kept to the rules. When in a jam with the police always smile, always remain calm and always tell the truth.

We wrote out statements with the assistance of most of the police force. They were fast becoming firm friends. Even the chief was thawing out. He was suspicious of Francesca because she had been in such an evident panic that she might betray her friends the Johnstones. She practically refused to utter a word about us. But he sidled over to me and suggested that if I found my husband serious about the blonde I might like to try a chief of police. A silly little twirp, while I was gazing at him wide-eyed asking for advice as to what to put in my statement, interrupted to tell me my eyes were too beautiful for words. We were getting along.

The guests wrote statements and I translated some of them. The only person who was really happy was the Finn. He sat down and wrote the story of his life and he was certain that he had found a public at last.

The evening wore on. Joao was fortifying himself with tenampa rum and we were scared he would get aggressive. So we suggested he teach some of the *pistoleros* how to play ping-pong. Francesca was grimly determined that if she had to go to jail she would do so on a full stomach, which meant that everyone else, including the fifteen members of the secret police, had to have their stomachs filled. So she stalked to and fro with cups of coffee and sandwiches and ignored all our efforts to brighten the party.

The party was very bright by this time. Everyone was certain that we were not the fifth column or whatever they were after and there were only a few formalities to finish up.

At last there was no possible excuse to delay their departure. We still did not know what they had come for. Finally light dawned when one of the men mentioned Trotsky. It seemed that we had all been in Mexico City on the day of the attempt. They had hopefully thought that we might have been involved. I thought that there must be other reasons. I asked the chief. He grinned.

'We have had information,' he said, and refused to explain why he had my name.

Before they left the chief called us together and made a handsome apology. We said we had loved it. Francesca said nothing. Then he asked if anyone had lost anything in the house. Francesca's maid said she had lost fifteen pesos out of the little *casita* where she slept. The chief produced fifteen pesos. The chief, with a little smile of boys will be boys, or rather, *pistoleros* will be *pistoleros*, produced another fifteen pesos. While he was talking, one of the policemen asked me to return his fountain pen which I had borrowed to sign my statement. I had returned it to someone exactly like him. I looked round and saw the man to whom I had returned the pen. I walked over and opened his coat. I lifted the pen gently out of his vest pocket.

'*Con su permiso?*' I murmured.

'*Cómo no,*' said the man, 'sure, sure.'

I returned the pen to the rightful owner.

The police went away. They left chaos behind. Archie and I were pleased with the whole business. We now had an in with the chief of the secret police, always useful in any country. Francesca was horrified. She had never gotten mixed up with police in her life. The guests were jittery and inclined to backbite and blame each other. We could not make them understand that it had been a fortunate incident.

There was only one thing still to be done. We had to find out just where and how these strange ideas about us had started.

The full investigation was carried on privately. Several factors became clear to us. We visited the chief of the police privately and he opened up considerably. The actual source of information was Mrs Halliday, a hysterical Mrs Halliday who declared that she was being menaced by the red terror. They also had some interesting information about Colin Bristow who had helped to excite Mrs Halliday by his conviction that I was an agent of the OGPU. Mrs Halliday was convinced that I was also a German agent because I did not wear a Union Jack in my hair or spit at Americans because they were not in the war.

I had no thought of being a sort of Mata Hari. But Colin's conviction that I was explained his strange behaviour. The police took all their information with reserve, but they had run up against a dead end in the Trotsky business and there was this 'Nest of International Spies' to be investigated. One newspaper went as far as to report the raid as a rain on a *'nido de espías internacionales'* across eight columns. The reporter wrote happily about *'damas elegantes'* and 'high-powered automobiles'. He mentioned a *'matrimonio de escritores'* which was presumably Archie and I, which I think deserves to enter the lists of gaggles of geese and partridges. We appeared again later as an American couple, the owners of the Hotel Quakero, in Madrid. Which just shows what an enterprising reporter can do with a story. We had told the police that we owned a hotel near Barcelona that was now being used by the Quakers. We still do not know who were the *damas elegantes*.

Colin left Cuernavaca. He went to Mexico City and stayed in a small hotel which was raided by Mexico City secret police. Colin was dismissed with a caution but it was too much. He left the country.

I ran across Mrs Halliday shortly before she too left Cuernavaca. She was going to Cuba. She eyed me with the fascination of a rabbit eyeing a snake. We met face to face in the middle of the sidewalk.

'Boo,' I said.

Oh-h-h-h,' she squealed and scuttled away. It was the only time I had ever spoken to her.

Chapter 21
Life in the *Quinta*

We settled down peacefully to life in our *quinta*. I had no desire to see any more foreigners. I had decided that everybody had been very stupid over the police business, except, of course, the Johnstones, and I could not be bothered to have anything more to do with them. Archie never wants to see foreigners at any time; he would rather get to know the natives of any country he is living in.

The trouble with living in Mexico is that the Mexicans do not want to know foreigners either. There is no getting away from the fact that Mexicans consider all foreigners as from the United States, and they are suspicious about people from the United States. They are perfectly civil and there are some who affect the mannerisms and even the language of the North Americans, but deep down Mexicans are not enthusiastic about foreigners.

When we first moved into the *quinta* the people living in the other little houses eyed us but did not respond to our greetings. They did not approve of the invasion. We had no idea what type of person lived in the *quinta*. We caught glimpses of husbands hurrying off to work, and as they wore suits and shoes we presumed that they had clerical jobs of some kind. The wives seemed to spend all day inside their houses and rarely visited each other. There were various children playing around who looked well cared-for.

I was given my first recognition after my first wash-day. Our house had an underground room like a cellar with a window and in it was my *lavadero*, the usual Mexican arrangement like a stone sink with a sloping floor and a tap. To wash sheets and white things the Mexicans scrub them with soap on the stone and then lay them full of suds flat in the sun to bleach. From time to time one flicks water over them so that they do not dry too quickly. When all the soap is dried out, the sheets are rinsed in clean water. I found that this was a marvellous way to get sheets white, and I duly stretched out my white wash on the grass slope outside my washroom. The neighbours were active that morning, passing and repassing my house on various errands and busily peeking at my wash. They watched and they saw. I might be a *gringa*, but at least I knew how to wash. One by one they wished me good morning. We were accepted in the *quinta*.

We found our neighbours pleasant. Behind us there lived a lawyer, an Indian with a wonderful mahogany face and thick grey hair. He had a young wife and two small daughters. He told us that he had studied in Paris and that he had a large practice among the country people. His house was his office and all day picturesque campesinos in their white cotton trousers and starched, pleated shirts wandered up to his door and sat down on the grass to wait for him. They sat on their haunches with their big sombreros pulled over their faces and would wait for hours without moving. Their disputes were mostly connected with just how long they were entitled to have the communal streams turned into their fields. One old lady was a regular visitor. She had loose black hair which hung around her dirt-encrusted face in greasy festoons. She wore a multitude of garments, all ample and made of different-coloured cottons. Over it all she draped an aged *rebozo*, or scarf. Her skirts were gathered into thick pleats and she wore at least six of them in different colours. Apparently she had some legal troubles, but she also came to sell eggs. She assured me that the señor lawyer was a wonderful man, so clever and so good. She had to bring him at least a dozen eggs every week.

I was fascinated buying eggs from her. She always approached with empty but grimy hands outspread. Would I care for any eggs? Even if I had a house full of eggs I had to say yes just to see what happened next. She fumbled in the folds of her *rebozo* and produced an egg. A large, white, fresh egg. I took it tenderly and put it in a dish. She lifted up one layer of skirt and produced something like a dirty cotton handkerchief from the pleats. Unwrapped, it revealed two eggs.

'*Ay, mamacita*' she would say. 'Ay, little mama, these are wonderful eggs. How many would you like?'

I could go on buying eggs all day. However, she dug around her waistband and brought forth three more. These she gave me. That was all. There were no more eggs. I longed to suggest that she shake herself just in case some had got left over from last week. I paid her the exact money, about 12 cents for six eggs. She beamed at me as she began to untie various knotted apron-strings among the masses of material below her neck. She appeared to sink deeper and deeper into what I had supposed to be her bosom but which seemed to consist mainly of old rags. Finally she produced another dirty handkerchief from somewhere in the recesses and unwrapped it carefully. She added the *centavos* to a small stock inside the handkerchief and the burrowing process went on again until the little hoard was enveloped safely and all the strings tied again in place. She shook me warmly by the hand and went away muttering that next week she would bring me more eggs, always supposing that she had a dozen for the good kind lawyer, who deserved to have fresh eggs every day.

To one side of us there lived a solitary old man who did not look like a Mexican. He turned out to be a Spaniard from Valencia who had lived most of his life in Mexico. He was amused by our attempts to make a garden round the house and helped us to combat the Cuernavaca plague, harvest ants. He had a wonderful liquid to pour down the ant holes which he explained, when set alight, exploded and made a gas which exterminated the ants. He was scornful of our efforts with ordinary disinfectant and would eagerly produce this wonderful liquid. The result was always embarrassing. The liquid would be poured down, Archie would get a stock with a piece of cotton soaked in alcohol, light it and apply it gingerly to the hole. The Valenciano would leap out of the way; mothers called to their children; I collected all the dogs I could see. We would wait. One minute, two minutes. Then the Valenciano would say it was most surprising. The stuff always made a terrific explosion in his field where he grew *pimientos*. He could not understand it at all.

A traveller for a firm of cracker had one of the houses for a part-time house. He and his family also had a house in Mexico City. They moved in after us with a large number of expensive flower pots. These they stacked up on their porch with a large sack full of something. We were interested in the sack. We could not guess what it could contain that could stand sunshine or rain without spoiling. We were soon on smiling terms with the traveller and his pretty wife—he was a devastatingly good-looking Mexican—and one day they asked if they could borrow my typewriter. My typewriter is old and my ambition is to be able to afford a Remington noiseless standard model, but for the moment the Corona is all I have. It means that Archie and I can afford to live where we please and even travel around occasionally. The poor thing even got blown up in Spain, but was rescued in working condition. I never lend my typewriter.

I was anxious to be on good terms with my neighbours and I wondered. I decided to break my rule. I would allow them to use my typewriter, but in my house. They came over with a sheaf of letters and the wife typed away while the beautiful traveller stalked up and down dictating. Later it became a nuisance to have them in the house and I said the hell with it and let them take the machine to their house. They did it no harm and later brought a machine of their own down from Mexico City. Much later, when Archie made a window box for our back porch, they gave us the contents of the sack—beautiful leaf mould which made our plants grow magnificently.

The lawyer confessed to us one day that he was really a poet. He had written several books of poetry, chiefly while he was in Paris, and we gathered the poems were gems of nostalgia. But he said that he could not support a family on poems, so he became a lawyer. He was tremendously proud of his pretty little wife, who trailed about the porch in satin robes with a beautiful blank face, spitting from time to time with perfect accuracy over the steps.

Another family, luckily living at some distance from us, consisted of Papa, Mama, and a bevy of children who looked vaguely all the same age and exactly alike. We counted up to about thirteen, but decided that they must have been running in circles. Eventually we found that there were seven only and we were fascinated trying to work out how on earth they, Papa, Mama and a maid managed to fit in the two-roomed house. Mama was enormously stout and wore flowing smocks and we were convinced that there would soon be an eighth child but the months wore on and Mama remained exactly the same. We concluded that she just always looked like that.

One night we were awakened by the sounds of a *marimba* band playing in the exact centre of the *quinta* at five o'clock in the morning. The band was banging away on an instrument like a wooden xylophone. We were told later that it was celebrating the arrival of the eighth child. We did not see Mama for some days, and then Archie came rushing in, in great excitement. He had seen Mama's back view on her porch and he declared she was twice the size. Archie is not given to exaggeration and I had to walk past the porch to investigate. I found that Mama's Mama had arrived to take charge and she was exactly like Mama, but on an even more generous scale.

Two of the little houses were empty. They were far removed from our house and we were not interested in their prospective tenants. We were glad to be on friendly terms with the people near us, otherwise we were going through one of the Johnstones' periodic phases. We were tired of seeing people and we were broke.

Archie's pupils were on their summer vacations, so there was no money coming in. We had a reserve, some of which we had intended to use for our own vacation. We had planned for months to take a trip up to the north of the West Coast. However, one of our friends had got into a jam and we used up most of our holiday money in a temporary loan. So we settled down to live on as little as possible.

Archie and I are peculiar in that we would always rather do our economizing before we are flat broke. I do not mind giving up luxuries like tea, drinks at the café, movies, when I know that we have enough money to live on for several months. I hate having to think every time I spend a cent unless I make it a kind of game. Archie would always rather go without anything than spend money. He is even upset if he gets an expensive present. He is not concerned about his money, he just hates to see money spent except on travelling.

I decided that we would spend four dollars a week on everything except the rent, which was about two dollars a week. I had a simple method of ensuring that we did not spend more than four dollars.

Every week I would put aside the money for the ice, newspapers, electric light, fuel. The rest of the money covered food, soap, razor blades, cigarettes, and odds and ends. There was usually about three dollars for this. I did the marketing at the beginning of the week, and if the money ran out before the week was out, we were out of luck. We went on native rations and waited until the days came round for the next four dollars. We never borrowed from one week to the next. Whenever went hungry. There was always rice, *masa* (a kind of dough made from ground corn), tomatoes and oranges. It was not a kind of life I would like to see stretching before me indefinitely, although I realized that even at our lowest we lived better than the people in the *jacales* across the road.

Our house was built on a promontory above the dirt road which ran parallel to the *barranca*. Between the road and the deep drop down to the water there was a little rough land sloping towards the edge of the cliff. Here and there little platforms had been made and huts built out of odd pieces of wood, flattened tin cans and shingling. The huts were flung together with no attempt to make the best of the poor materials, and no one bothered to make a window. Cooking was done outside the door on a portable brazier, the inhabitants squatting on the dust earth. The people lived in good-natured or apathetic proximity to each other, to draggled chickens tied by their legs to doorposts, to pigs half buried in the dust, to dogs and cats prowling around for food. At night everything alive went into the one room of the hut and the door was stoutly shut. Everything came out alive in the morning.

We could watch the life in the *jacales* from our front terrace. At first I was horrified to think people could be so poor in a prosperous town like Cuernavaca. Then I began to realize that, although the people were poor enough, a little thought and ingenuity without any expense could improve the huts out of all recognition. I watched one being built. Two lads put it up in a morning. They had plenty of materials and they slapped one piece of wood upon another with no attempt to fit them together. They patched up the roof with tins, but they did not bother to make them overlap to keep out the rain. It dawned on me that they simply did not care. They would have liked more food, but otherwise they retired into their huts securely wrapped in some odd mysticism of their own which allowed them to ignore the rain or the heat. It showed clearly why Mexico is far more Indian than Spanish. It is possible to break something rigid, but not something that bends indefinitely. The Indians have bent before the Conquest, quietly and patiently, and they have gone right on living exactly as before.

Cuernavaca is a good example of the position of Indians in Mexico. Cuernavaca is a resort, a weekend rest resort for rich Mexicans from Mexico City. It is also a tourist centre. Most of the large stores are run by Gachupines, Spanish-Mexicans who speak exaggerated lisping *castellano*.

The *zócalo* any day at any hour is thick with *sombreros*;

the white cottons of the *campesinos*; the gay pink cottons of their wives. It is knee deep in Indians. The squares, the Cathedral gardens, the streets, are thronged with Indians. They do not live in the centre of the town, they come in from the country districts on horseback, the women sitting precariously sideways, or they live in huts along the *barranca*. But they come to Cuernavaca and fill the place. Tourists have to push their way through them, Mexicans from Mexico City have to screech their motor horns to clear them out of the streets. The Indians belong there. They may call the place Cuernavaca after the first Spaniards who could not pronounce the Náhuatl name, but to the Indians it is still Cuahnahuac, 'Near Wooded Mountains'.

Chapter 22
She Calls Herself Alhambra

There was some excitement in our *quinta* when No 7 was taken. It was a blue house across the central garden and we watched the move with some amusement. To begin with there was a piano, which was unusual, but the house was far enough away for us not to be apprehensive about the piano. It was the sigh of the new owner, a good-looking Mexican apparently disguised as a Marseilles waterfront man, lifting a large trunk and the superintendent of the *quinta* up the front steps that amused us. The superintendent though he was helping by hanging on to one end but he never got a chance to keep his feet on the ground.

I think I was the last person in the *quinta* to realize that the Mexican's wife was American, north American. I resented it. Here we had moved to an exclusively Mexican community to get away from foreigners and now north Americans were crowding us out. I complained to Archie that Mexico was getting simply impossible. We would have to move into the interior or even to Chile. I toyed lovingly with the idea of moving to Chile. Archie was not alarmed. We had only just enough money to keep us going in Mexico until the children's vacations were over. We did have a small reserve of dollars which we refused to touch—strictly it wasn't ours—and we had lent the money we had saved for our own vacation. Archie knew that for the moment we could not go to Chile.

On the terrace of No 7 the following conversation was taking place in English:

'Jack, what nationality *is* that woman in No 1?'

Jack grunted. He was wrestling with some problems of stress and strain.

'You know, I believe she must be German. She certainly isn't English. The English don't walk freely like that.'

'Huh,' said Jack, unsatisfactorily.

'She is certainly blonde enough for a German. I guess she must be German. But her husband doesn't look German at all.'

'Why, Periquita,' exclaimed Jack suddenly. 'There's my Butchie. He must be hungry, the poor cat. Listen to how he cries. Butchie, Butchie. You know, he gets more beautiful every day.'

'Jack, I don't believe you have heard a single word of what I've been saying.'

'About the people in No 1? It doesn't matter. We don't have to know them.'

Archie was saying: 'Even if the new family *is* half *gringo* we don't have to know it.'

So we forgot the people in No 7. I was thankful they lived all the way across the garden because they had a steady stream of American friends who poured down for weekends. The man of the house might be a Mexican, but it was an American household. Foreigners had invaded the *quinta*.

We were invaded in another fashion. Dogs found us out. Mexican dogs have certain mental characteristics in common, if no physical ones. They all appear to have the sweetest dispositions, they invariably lie with their front paws crossed, and they all want to be owned. They are mostly hungry, but more important even than food is to belong to someone.

In Mexico City the dogs gang up on the unwary in the

Alameda park. Archie and I were passing through the centre of the park about one o'clock in the morning when we were rushed by a pack of dogs. There were about twelve of them, every size and shape and utterly unrecognizable as any particular breed. The leading dog, a pleasant-looking object with a bit of Alsatian in him a long way back, reached us and turned to face the others. He planted himself before us and dared the others to come on. He practically said, 'Scram, boys, they're mine.' The others trotted off, some lingering hopefully near by, and the dog proceeded to greet us as if we were old friends. He gave a beautiful demonstration of a long-lost pet returned to the bosom of the family. He licked our faces, leaped madly round us, and finally trotted a little ahead of us, his ears and tail up, his strut an eloquent commentary on his new status. We strolled through the park and sat for a while on one of the stone benches. The dog lay at our feet, only stirring once to chase away an impudent dog who came too close. When we moved on he came with us, keeping close to our heels. We noticed that he was not hungry-looking. The other dogs in the pack looked, too, as if they found enough to keep their ribs reasonably well-covered. It was plain that the idea was to find an owner, not to beg scraps of food.

We felt terrible. We could not take him back to our hotel and in any case we did not want another dog. It seemed cruel to have to disappoint him when he was so sure that he was owned at last. We got rid of him near the hotel by diving up side alleys in opposite directions. I could seen him from the window of our room dashing up and down the street trying to locate us. He stayed nearly an hour, searching desperately and then went back to the park to try again.

We could duck the dogs in Mexico City. In the *quinta* they had us at bay.

We ate on our back porch and the dogs would collect on the steps. Yellow dogs, brown dogs, long dogs, short dogs, every conceivable kind of dog, sat on their bony haunches and eyed every mouthful we ate. We knew it would be fatal to feed them but sometimes it was impossible to resist those gentle, hungry eyes. We threw scraps as far away from the house as possible. There was one white terrier bitch who was a marvel at snitching food out of the other dogs' mouths. She had obviously just had puppies and was pathetically thin, every bone showing under her dirty white coat. We concentrated on throwing more food to her than to the others because she was in such bad condition. She was scared to have us come near her but she watched us with bright brown eyes and never missed anything we threw.

Biscuit had disappeared. He was with us for a month after we moved and then he was stolen. He had turned into a beautiful dog, still only a puppy, but he had filled out and was going to be very good-looking. There was a tendency to steal puppies in Cuernavaca, presumably to sell elsewhere because Cuernavaca was overrun with hungry, homeless dogs. The people liked the fun of having a pretty little pup and then neglected it when it grew up.

We were without a dog of our own although we certainly did not lack dogs. One day I was piqued by the obvious terror of the white bitch. I spent nearly an hour coaxing her to let me touch her. I touched her black head and she suddenly gave a leap into my lap.

'My God, Archie,' I said. 'We've got another dog.'

We washed her and were surprised to find that, except for her thinness, she was the exact counterpoint of the dog in the 'His Master's Voice' trademark. She was just what I loathe in a dog. I hate smooth-haired fox terriers, I hate bitches, I hate white dogs. Archie did not care for her either but he can resign himself to almost anything. For a long time we used to disclaim ownership. When she went to Archie I would say, 'You know, she's your dog really. How sweet.' The next moment she would run to me and Archie would remark, 'All animals adore you. She is *your* dog.'

She had no name. She was not allowed inside the house. She put on weight and her coat shone. She was extremely clever. She never pushed her attentions but she was always there when one of us reached out for an absent-minded hand. She took to coming round to the front terrace and we gave up noticing. Suddenly it dawned on us that she was a dog of some pretensions to race. She was undoubtedly a smooth-haired fox-terrier. She took to sleeping on the couch on the front terrace.

Several weeks after the terrier had adopted us I was in the local store getting bread. The terrier was with me. She still had no name. Neither Archie nor I would admit that she was now absolutely our dog. An old Indian woman muffled in her *rebozo* made some remark about the dog.

'Yes, she is a nice looking dog,' I agreed.
'She is called Alhambra,' remarked the old woman.
'I beg your pardon?' I said. 'She is called what?'
'Alhambra,' said the old woman.
'Well, how do you know?' I asked.
'She is my dog,' said the old woman.
'She seems to be my dog now,' I said. 'Why didn't you feed her?'

The old woman shrugged. 'We have so many dogs,' he said. Then she collected her packages. '*Con permiso*,' she said and shuffled away. I bought my bread and turned to go. 'Come on, Alhambra,' I said.

Alhambra sensed a new security with her name. She took to visiting Archie in the mornings and after licking whatever part of his face was visible, she would curl up and go to sleep on his bed.

Alhambra was firmly established in the house when we found Biscuit. We were walking through the next little village when a huge yellow dog nearly knocked us flat. It was Biscuit, looking wonderful, well-fed and crazy with excitement at seeing us again. He was with a man and a little boy who were collecting fruit. Biscuit settled down to follow us home. We asked the man to hold him. The man seemed to think we were absurd but he held him while we walked away. We decided that as Biscuit had such a good home it was kinder to leave him there.

Biscuit had other ideas. I was awakened the following morning by heavy breathing outside the screening and there was Biscuit. He had decided to come home.

Alhambra was furious. She did not care for the intrusion. But she accepted it and settled down, although Biscuit was given to understand that it was her home and he was merely tolerated in it. We were pleased to have him back partly because he was such a charming dog but also because he chased away all the other dogs from around the house.

The people in No 7 also got a dog. It was an extraordinary looking little object, vaguely black and white with a tiny worried face and an ear-splitting bark. We were more thankful than ever that No 7 was as far away as possible in the *quinta*.

Chapter 23
Jack Has Some Gossip

Archie suddenly got the offer of a job on a new English page running in a Mexican paper. It meant working in Mexico City, and it meant working. We seriously considered turning it down. I have the firm belief that Archie should consider his steady-job days over. Archie is not reluctant to agree, but he also likes to think of a convenient sum of money put away for emergencies. We do not know what these emergencies may be, anything from a trip around Mexico to a sudden dash back to Spain, but undoubtedly there always are emergencies. Archie decided to take the job for a time and to save as much of his salary as he could manage. Then, when we had enough put by, he would quit and we could look around for something amusing to do.

We had got acquainted with our foreign neighbours. The girl was American and the man Mexican. He had lived twenty years in the United States and had somehow acquired a cross between an Italian and a Scandinavian accent. It was baffling to hear him say 'yumping' and 'lika dis' in the same breath. For some time I did not understand a single word except when he spoke Spanish, and my first impressions of Jack were wrapped in a haze of immense good humour and incoherence.

Ella was the sort of person I had been looking for. She had in many ways the same sort of outlook as I have. We found that we could discuss interminably and enjoy ourselves enormously. I found a feminine mind a great relief after being almost exclusively with men, especially a feminine mind that did not deal entirely in personalities.

When we got acquainted with Ella and Jack we also met their livestock. Chulita was the weird little dog with the shrill bark. She obviously had pom antecedents with perhaps a dash of terrier. The result was a tiny, wizened face, bright black eyes, an inquisitive nose that was never still, a fluffy black and white coat, a broad chest with sturdy front legs, a high back with long back legs, and a tremendous straight tail with fringes on it. She was bossy and busy and had to supervise every movement of everyone, but somehow managed to have a great charm in spite of the bark.

Butch was a magnificent grey Persian cat. He was Jack's pride and joy and no one dared to criticize him, although Ella and I had a suspicion that he was an extremely dumb cat. Chulita gave him hell at meal times, so Jack insisted that Butch (who was twice Chulita's size) should have his meals on the kitchen window sill. Ella came to the conclusion that Butch was not too bright when, after the hundredth time he was shown, he could not grasp that his food was on the window sill. When she at last lifted him up to it, he would mew gently and drop the choicest bits of meat on the floor, where Chulita snapped them up. But Butch was handsome; there was no argument about that.

Our two families caused a certain amount of chat in the *quinta*. Apparently all foreigners had the strangest habits. Instead of having children, they busied themselves with animals and flowers. Their husbands left them for weeks on end. While other wives stayed at home and minded the children, the foreigners went out on their own, entertained men friends, and most extraordinary, did their own housework. In spite of our peculiarities, Ella and I were good friends with the rest of the *quinta,* and our gardens were much admired.

Archie settled down to his work in Mexico City. He found himself a comfortable furnished room for five dollars a month. There was room for me to stay with him when I went up for shopping. He was much happier than when working on *The Good Neighbour*.

Archie laughed at me when I said that I was sure *The Good Neighbour* would yet materialize. I could not see Hiram in the role of failure. Most people said that obviously Hiram had realized that it could never come off and had decided to stay in New York. No one seemed quite sure what had happened to Rafael, but the general opinion was that he was in jail.

It was during Archie's first weekend back in Cuernavaca that Hiram walked in. He just strolled up on our terrace as if he had been away a few weeks. He seemed embarrassed by our surprise.

'I don't know what you are all talking about,' he said. 'There was never any doubt about *The Good Neighbour*.'

'When we didn't hear—' began Archie.

'What do you mean, didn't hear? I answered all your letters.'

The concerted howl was too much even for Hiram.

'Well, most of them,' he said. 'Of course, I was travelling about and some letters may have gone astray.'

'Have a drink and tell us all about it.'

'How is Rafael?' I asked sweetly.

When Hiram got over his choking fit, we gathered that he was not speaking to Rafael any more. Rafael was a rat. Hiram, it seemed, had always had doubts about Rafael. The whole delay (Hiram admitted that there had been some delay) was due to Rafael. In fact, Rafael stank.

Hiram was hurt that Archie had shown such little faith.

After all, he had promised to bring out *The Good Neighbour* and it should have been obvious that the delays were just one of those things. When Hiram set out to do anything—I interrupted.

'Hiram, your moustache? Have you shaved it off?'

'What do you mean? Of course I haven't shaved it off.'

'Sorry. I see it now. It was the light or something.'

'I'm not going to shave it off until the edition is out. Then I'll get rid of the damn thing.'

'Don't forget to tell us,' I said.

'Just what are your plans about the edition?' asked Archie.

Hiram plunged into details about advertising, raising money. Archie explained that it seemed impossible to get any advertising.

'Nonsense,' said Hiram. 'I've been thinking it over. If we pay our space sellers some of their commission, say 25 per cent, when they bring in the ads, they'll bring them in all right.'

'Good God,' said Archie. 'Of course they will. But that is just the point. You can't pay them anything until the ads are paid for.'

'We've got to,' said Hiram. 'I think I can fix it. I shall explain to the backers that it is their only chance of pulling off the edition. I've only come back to get the backers' money back for them. I don't suppose I shall make a cent out of it myself.'

'I always said Hiram had noble instincts,' I said.

Hiram glared at me and then burst out laughing.

'Well,' I said triumphantly when Hiram had gone. 'I told you *The Good Neighbour* wasn't entirely lost.'

'Certainly you were right about Hiram,' said Archie, 'but I'll believe in that edition when I see it.'

With Archie in Mexico City for two weeks at a stretch, I should have had time on my hands but, although I missed him, I was occupied every moment. I had a letter from my British publishers, to whom I had sent a manuscript of a novel six months previously, to say they intended publishing in the spring of 1941. I had almost forgotten sending the manuscript. I thought either the ship taking it over had been sunk or the publishers had been put out of business by bombs. As it was, the poor things had had a time-bomb fall in their offices and they had to move out temporarily while the bomb either exploded or was removed. Luckily it was removed and they moved right back into their offices and went on working. The news that they were publishing was a surprise. I had washed out the British market altogether. I immediately rang up Archie to suggest he quit work. He said a bomb might yet blow the market sky-high and he would keep right on working.

The letters we got from England showed that there is not much difference between bombed Spaniards and bombed British. They both became furious and grimly determined. The British superiority of active defence was balanced by the better shelters of the Spaniards. When we were in England in 1938 for a few months, we were horrified to find that the British Government had no intention of providing deep shelters. They also intended to prohibit the use of the subways. Apparently for one the British people took matters into their own hands and invaded the subways and the British *Daily Worker* led a successful campaign for better shelters. But obviously the shelters were nothing like the underground fortresses in Madrid.

Bombs seem to be the chief topic of conversation among elderly ladies in the country districts. A friend of mine wrote that the local Red Cross meetings were practically a shambles in the battle to relate each one's experience. Finally one old lady rapped on the table and said shortly, 'Well, we must get this settled. Shall I tell about *my* bomb or will you tell about *your* bomb?'

I worked on the manuscript in the mornings and afternoons and took the dogs out in the evenings. We walked for miles and I always wished mildly that I had a horse. I walk if I must and if there is no other way of getting exercise or seeing the country, but I have always preferred riding. In Spain I did not miss it because it was not good riding country and there was always swimming to make up for it. But Mexico screams for a horse. There are long sandy rides along the ridges between the *barrancas* with view of the snow-covered mountains, grassy tracks between fields of sugar cane or across rice fields. I had once or twice hired a horse, but the hirelings were poor and the price high. There did not seem to be much chance of owning a horse and paying for its keep.

The evenings I usually spent with Ella and Jack or they came down to my house. Usually it was just Ella, because Jack was often away. They were going through a bad spot and I could sympathize with them, knowing bad spots myself. The difference was that bad spots to Archie and me meant something devastating like the Spanish war or losing everything we had, and invariable the Johnstone luck producing something to compensate us. Ella and Jack just seemed to be dogged by a series of unfortunate incidents, starting with a smash-up of the lorry in which Jack was bringing all their possessions from the United States to Mexico. That little misfortune meant Jack was knocked unconscious; a number of valuables, including mining machinery, were stolen by the rescuers; Jack became mixed up in an involved Mexican lawsuit; and the whole incident seemed to start off a landslide of small misfortunes.

Jack and Ella never complained. They just tossed off from time to time some remark that such and such a thing was lost in the wreck, or that so and so had swindled them, or that that was the time when Ella was sick. Then questioning would discover that the thing lost in the wreck was machinery valued at several thousand pesos which Jack had been counting on to sell; that they had been swindled out of large sums, and that the time Ella was sick she had nearly died.

Archie and I suddenly discovered why we like Ella and Jack so much. They were extraordinarily happy together. So were Archie and I. It was a relief to be with a couple who liked one another. Most of our friends were either separated, about to be separated, or wishing to hell they could be separated. They looked on us as something slightly abnormal. It was a pleasure to be with people as abnormal as ourselves.

Mexico does seem to attract peculiar people. The rather self-conscious attitude automatically adopted by foreigners among a different race seems to accentuate peculiarities. There is always gossip and chatter in small communities, but nowhere have I found such bitterness and viciousness as in the Mexican gossip. The Harpies think out and stage their own gossip, creating situations where there are none. The white-headed Vultures of Mexico sail around waiting for the scraps, which they rend and tear among themselves until the original victim is unrecognizable.

Ella and I both enjoy what *we* call gossip. I was the first to inform Ella that my neighbour had come home drunk and had beaten up his wife, who consequently wore dark glasses for days. We were mostly interested in the fact that the wife did nothing about it. We had a nice cosy chat about what we would do in similar circumstances. Ella rushed to tell me that her neighbour's maid had dressed up in her master's clothes and had paraded all round the terrace when her mistress was away and we had a happy speculation about the goings-on generally. Archie listens to this sort of thing with a tolerant smile; Jack looks blank and cannot see why anyone should bother to talk about anything so uninteresting. Archie has been known to remember something amusing about someone to tell me; Jack would not register it for a moment. Ella and I attacked Jack severely one day about this inability to remember gossip.

'But gossip is nothing,' expostulated Jack. 'How can I remember dis and dat which is nothing?'

'You might try,' we said. 'You are always poring over your engineering books and you can remember all sorts of stuff out of them.'

'Oh, facts,' said Jack. 'Of course I can remember facts.'

However, Jack had the sweetest nature. He was genuinely anxious to oblige us. One day he came back from Mexico in a state of great excitement.

'Listen,' he cried. 'I have some gossip.'

'No!' we shrieked. We wondered which of our friends had been doing what.

'It was at Tres Marías,' said Jack, mentioning a bleak village between Mexico City and Cuernavaca. 'The bus stopped for a long time. Something had been happening in Tres Marías. There had been sent six tax collectors to collect the taxes and the men of Tres Marías do not like to pay taxes. So they take the six tax collectors and they shoot the six tax collectors dead. There, dat is gossip for you.'

Chapter 24
Pride of the Penitentiary

We had been more than a year in Mexico. I was amused when I recalled my first reaction to the country. Archie had been perfectly right to like the place from the start. We would still prefer to go back to our house in Spain if the political situation changed. The little news we had from Spain was depressing except for the fact that our old staff was still being employed by the people who had taken the place over. Various anxious friends suggested we should make the property over to an American because of Spain's attitude in the war, but we decided not to worry. We could never go back unless the régime changed, and we knew that under a left régime we should have no difficulty in establishing our claim to live on our property at any rate. We were thankful that our old staff were employed, which meant that they, at least, would get enough to eat.

I have never had any idea of settling permanently in Mexico. Perhaps in the present conditions the idea of settling permanently anywhere seems to be a joke. But Mexico takes a lot of beating as a country to live in. There were the usual scare stories about the Mexican elections— the American press loves scare stories about Mexico—and there were some unpleasant articles written about the way the election was pulled, but in fact there was about as much difference between the candidates as there was between Roosevelt and Willkie. Many of the *campesinos*, landworkers, supported Almazán because he had promised them his support over the land question; so had Ávila Camacho. Many of the *gachupines*, the Spanish storekeepers, supported Almazán because they had promised to do down the *campesinos*. The only important point in the elections was the attitude of the United States. There were people who believed that the United States might support a Right uprising by Almazán, but the general opinion was that the United States would suddenly wake up to the fact that she needed a friendly neighbour. Which she did with a bang, and the New York press even piped down, dismissing the demonstrations at Wallace's visit as 'unimportant'. Mexico seemed to be settling back for a minor boom with United States capital, and perhaps this time Mexico might profit by it.

Ella's attitude to Mexico differed from mine. She was married to a Mexican and considered Mexico her country. She wanted to settle here. The only trouble was what she was to settle with.

Jack had been trying to get any kind of a job, but with the unsettled conditions before the elections it was impossible. Everything has to be done through pull in Mexico and at election time no one is doing any pulling—he is waiting to be pushed. The situation seemed pretty hopeless. Ella could not live in Mexico City, where she could get work, because the altitude made her sick. Jack was running himself ragged trying to wangle something. I suddenly had an idea which at least helped the situation. I suggested that they give up their house and move in with me.

Archie thought I had gone crazy when I told him. He knows how I like being alone and how I dislike people about the house, but he did not know Ella very well. I knew that she and I had as good a chance as any two people of sharing a house. Jack would be away a great deal and Archie only came down for alternate weekends. We decided to take the chance.

Moving day was a surprise. Jack suddenly decided to moving in while he was still there to help. I had friends over the weekend and was busy. I saw occasional glimpses of Jack staggering across the *quinta* with enormous pieces of furniture on his back and heard Ella's protests when he tried to take too much. I had handed them over our bedroom and the storeroom downstairs for Jack's tools and the extra furniture that would not fit into the house. I decided to move to Mexico City while they settled in. When I returned it was like a transformation scene. My kitchen, always sparsely furnished, was bursting with pots and pans and waffle makers; the back porch had a cupboard and a new table; the front porch had a new couch. It was all most satisfactory. Only Chulita's bark was superfluous.

I gave that small dog hell. Every time she raised a sound I beat her. I never let up. After a week she made less noise than a mouse. But she had to show her independence. If a stranger walked through the *quinta* she would rush up to me to attract my attention. Then she would sit down, cock up one ear, look at me out of the corners of her eyes and let out the ghost of a yap. Oddly enough she was fond of me in spite of my discipline. I asked Ella if she minded me beating her dog and she said she wanted to do it herself but she was too tired.

Alhambra, my fat terrier, accepted the invasion philosophically. She was good friends with Chulita but she found it difficult to adjust herself to Butch. I had encouraged her to chase a persistent black cat that was always trying to steal things out of the kitchen and she took a little time to learn the difference between a black cat and a grey cat. But she did learn, just as she learned another impossible rule—that she could jump on my bed when there was a cover on it and not otherwise. Alhambra might have been a peculiar figure, but she had brains.

It was partly to improve Alhambra's figure that I decided that I must find a horse to ride. Alhambra had changed from a skimpy, starving misery into a buxom matron with round, gleaming white sides. The Johnstone fortunes were looking up and I felt I could afford to hire a horse occasionally. The trouble was to find one worth hiring. Eventually I found a good little horse just up the road from my house. He cost about 45 cents an hour to hire, which was expensive, but I was assured that he was a very well-known horse in the village of Acapatzingo, where he won all the races in the penitentiary. I felt that such a horse was worth paying 45 cents an hour for. One never knew when one might want to win a race in the penitentiary.

He turned out to be a fine little horse, very keen and fast and sure-footed enough for the rough roads. I was so excited to be riding again that poor Ella suffered considerably and went to be to dream of hocks and withers, fetlocks and pasterns. Ella prided herself on knowing nothing whatever about animals. She had to admit that her New York superiority was spoiled in Mexico, where she could not help learning a fair amount about scorpions, centipedes, and *garapatas*, crab-like creatures which get into dogs' coats. But she thought he would stick to her ignorance of quadrupeds over dog size. Poor Ella.

Jack came back from a mysterious trip into the interior. He was bursting with excitement and his good-looking face had lost the drawn look from hunting jobs. He had a job. There were still some preliminaries to be settled and it might take a while before he could start, but he had a job. A swell job. He eyed Ella in a comic way. There were snags. He would have to live right out in the interior, miles from civilization. It would be tough going. Ella interrupted.

'I suppose all this means you are mixed up with a mine somewhere.'

Jack laughed. It was the first time I heard him laugh and sound carefree.

'No,' he said. 'This is different. This time I am going to work on a cattle ranch.'

I left them discussing the pros and cons. It sounded wonderful. I was sorry for Ella having to be without Jack for a time while he started work. He would have to live out in the wilds overseeing some big herds down in Guerrero, where the climate was hot and there were no civilized comforts. He would sleep in the wilds and eventually either be moved to another location where Ella might come, or attempt to make some sort of living place wherever he was sent. It seemed that it would be several months before he knew definitely where his headquarters would be. I knew Ella would hate being without him, but I was glad that she could stay with me. I was trying to think of some way of compensating for this separation when they called me into their room. Ella was sitting on the bed, her dark hair on end, her blue eyes shining.

'I've decided to got with him,' she said. 'We are going to live in a tree.'

'Why a tree?' I asked, falling into a chair.

'I am scared to death of insects,' explained Ella solemnly. 'It is no use sleeping *under* a tree because they drop on one. So we shall live *up* the tree. Insects can't fall upwards.'

We talked for hours and grew more and more hysterical. Jack decided to make a concrete floor with lime around it and to make a rough construction to hang screening from. Ella insisted that she wanted a tree. Jack said that the trees were all stunted in Guerrero. Ella said she would have a stunted tree. I caused a diversion by pointing out that Jack would have to build a window-sill for Butch, who had just learned where to find his food. That meant building a window, which was awkward without any walls. Ella repeated that she had been right when she wanted to live in a tree. Butch would have to learn it all over again.

In spite of our hilarity, we all realized just what going into the interior with Jack meant to Ella. She was completely New York. She had never lived even in settled country. She was going to live in the hot lands with the nearest water from the Balsas river, a mile away. She was going to live among mosquitos and she would have to wear boots because of little insects in the dust which creep under one's toe nails. She would not even have a hut to live in at the start. Until Jack had an idea of where he would be able to settle, which would not be for some months, there was no money to waste building permanent homes. Jack was a pioneer; he thought nothing of sleeping on the ground among the scorpions. He suggested that Ella wait a while.

'Listen,' said Ella. 'I married you, didn't I? I'm tired of having a husband away all the time. I'm coming with you and we'll live in a tree. I can learn. I have always learned to light the boiler for the hot water by myself.'

Jack laughed. 'There won't be any boiler for hot water in a tree.'

'How do you know?' said Ella. 'If I know you, you'll have a complete hot water system built in a few months. There is nothing like being prepared.'

The Harpies and Vultures were charmed with the idea.

'Of course she can't trust him away from her.'

'N-no. Except that he *is* away a good deal.'

'There must be a *reason* for burying herself in that God-forsaken spot.'

'Perhaps she really *likes* being with her husband—'

'Don't be so absurd. What an idea! Why the man is a Mexican.'

Mrs Willoughby-Houghton thought it was wonderful. 'My dear, so brave. We think it is splendid of you.'

'Far from the madding crowd,' murmured Hamilton Rice. 'Not for me, I fear. I should miss my little treasures, you know.'

'I can't think what all the fuss is about,' said Ángel tartly. 'After all, I spent four weeks at Pie de la Cuesta beach at Acapulco living in a hovel and no one thought anything of it. And if you could have seen those pigs—'

I told Hiram about the idea. He was not interested because he had not thought of it himself.

'I'm going down there with them,' I said. 'I think it is a good story.'

'Nothing in it,' said Hiram. 'They just sound nuts to me.'

Hiram was working night and day on *The Good Neighbour*. He had wrenched more money out of the backers; he had whipped up an efficient team of space-sellers. The ads were coming in and *The Good Neighbour* seemed all set.

'You see how it is,' he said to Archie. 'It was perfectly easy to get the ads. It just needed a little confidence.'

'And good space-sellers and a lot more money,' said Archie.

The Good Neighbour was scheduled for publication three weeks ahead and Hiram no longer appeared for weekends. We heard rumours of frantic hard work. Most of the promised articles failed to appear until the last possible moment, which meant that Hiram had to do a last minute translation job as well as fill in with editorials and do the make-up. We heard that Hiram was looking ghastly and was on the verge of a breakdown. Then there was complete silence. Publication day passed, three more weeks went by and suddenly one Saturday Hiram walked in carrying a copy of *The Good Neighbour* under his arm.

'Here it is,' he said and slumped into a chair.

He certainly looked a wreck. His face was greenish-grey, his eyes were bloodshot. Ella came in and stared at him.

'You look different,' she said.

'He looks dead,' I said.

In a couple of days he had recovered sufficiently to start talking about a new project, but there was something odd about him. He seemed depressed and we would catch him eyeing us in a furtive way. At last we met Hamilton Rice at the Universal Café.

'Why, Hiram,' said Hamilton Rice. 'You've removed your moustache. How you young men change around from one day to the next.'

Chapter 25
Life, Death and Terry

I suddenly decided to take a holiday. It seemed absurd to be living in a country like Mexico and not to have seen anything except round Cuernavaca, Mexico City and Vera Cruz. I suggested that my American publishers should do something about it. They came across nobly.

Whenever I suggested to Archie that he get a couple of weeks off and come with me on a trip, he always produced objections. I thought he was reluctant to spend his hard-earned money, so I bounced in with a cheque and much enthusiasm. Archie still seemed unenthusiastic. Then I discovered that Archie's idea of a perfect holiday was to come home to Cuernavaca, eat plenty of home-cooked food, and sleep in the sun. So I decided to take a holiday alone.

I decided to go to Oaxaca, because most people from Cuernavaca had gone to Guadalajara, which is in the opposite direction. Oaxaca state is bounded on the south by the Pacific Ocean, with the port of Salina Cruz, and on the east by the state of Chiapas, a little-explored region of Mexico. The romantic town of Tehuantepec, noted for its picturesque and dominating women, is in Oaxaca and I wanted to visit it, but I decided that I would wait until Archie felt like taking a trip. I went to the town of Oaxaca, a supposedly twelve-hour railway journey from Puebla.

It was my second railroad journey in Mexico. The first was from Vera Cruz to Mexico City when we arrived eighteen months before. I had learned a lot. Then we travelled pullman from Vera Cruz and we had eyed with horror the odd-looking foods sold by the wayside. This time I took a second-class ticket. As soon as the second-class compartment is full, everyone overflows into the first class. I did not even wait for the overflowing to start. Leaving Puebla at 6.30 am it was perishingly cold. I wrapped myself in my great-coat and tied a sweater round my feet. An Indian woman came through the train with hot coffee and *tamales*, ground corn flavoured with chile and steamed in maize husks. She had only two pitchers, which everyone drank out of, and it would have been all the same to me if she had had only one pitcher. The coffee was excellent and the *tamales* at least made a warm poultice inside.

I made only one serious error on that journey. The seats had movable backs for facing either way, and I pushed over the back of the seat ahead of me in order to make a footrest. This was taken as an invitation to everyone to sit down to entertain me. It was swell for a time, but I have a great facility for sleeping in railroad trains, however uncomfortable, and the effort of keeping awake to explain for the tenth time that I was not a *gringa*, a *norte-americana*, that it did always rain in my country, that the war in Europe was terrible, that Europe was miles away across the sea and not part of the United States, that I thought Mexico was swell, was exhausting.

The journey was beautiful, through a series of mountain passes and valleys with hillsides apparently covered with still-looking trees which turned out to be enormous organ cactuses. We stopped for lunch at a little station crowded with women carrying eatables. Everyone in the train got out except for an American couple who looked pleasant but bewildered. I did not dare talk to them for fear of being landed with them all the way to Oaxaca. I noticed they had brought their own lunch and seemed perfectly happy. They were puzzled by me and my various friends on the train and when I retuned to my seat carrying fried *tortillas*, *enchiladas* and *tamales,* I heard the man say:

'You are quite right. She can't be American. Look at what she is going to eat!'

'What on earth are they?' asked the woman.

'I don't know but I took a look at them at the station and they were covered with flies.'

'May you never find anything worse,' I said silently to myself as I had a wonderful meal.

I think newcomers to Mexico should be careful what they eat. The Mexican passion for fingering food horrified me when I first came. But I think after a while one builds up a resistance to infection. Certainly I should have picked up something during my stay in Oaxaca if I had not been pretty tough.

My chief idea was to get out of Oaxaca as soon as possible. It is a charming town with a peculiarly pleasant, soft atmosphere of contentment, but I do not like staying in towns if I can help it. The first day of my arrival I discovered one Don Luis Montes who had a stable.

Don Luis was like a caricature of a Mexican. He had a fat, good-natured face, wore a huge *charro sombrero* with silver decorations, chin strap under his nose, a decorated shirt tied in a knot over an enormous paunch, which was pushed and squeezed into the tightest pair of surprisingly well-shaped but bowed legs. He was violently good-natured and a shrewd judge of a horse. He had some good horses, including two giants of over seventeen hands high. These were the horses of the Governor. Don Luis himself was some relation to the Governor. He promised to let me ride the big horses.

My first ride was up a mountain back of Oaxaca and for the first time I realized what a beautiful place it was. The town lies in a valley, or rather in the intersections of several valleys, surrounded by *sierras* on *sierras*. The mountains look as if they had been pinched out of *papier-mâché* by a giant fresh from Art School. It was the dry season and everything was bare, which showed off the planes and surfaces of the hills and gave a precision to the outlines of the piled up mountains behind. Soft sandy roads stretched up the valleys in all directions. It was a horseback rider's paradise.

I persuaded Don Luis to let me take a horse to Mitla for several days. He was worried because I refused to take a *mozo* with me to look after the horse. I assured him I was perfectly capable of looking after a horse. He said it was not that, but that a German had once hired a horse to ride down to Tehuantepec and he had refused to take a *mozo* and he had simply ridden away and never returned. I said I was leaving my typewriter behind in my boarding house and that a typewriter was worth far more than his horse. In the course of a heated discussion we drank a lot of beer and he agreed to trust me with his horse. He was slightly doubtful if I should find my way. But agreed that there was a highway, even if a rather bad one. I did not tell him I had no intention of staying on the highway.

Mitla is about thirty miles from Oaxaca along the new highway, which is only partly built, although buses do get along it. I took the country roads leading through the many small villages. These roads were sandy and perfect for riding and my horse was keen and fresh. We stopped whenever we felt like a rest and I drank beer when there was beer to be got or drank water with complete rashness out of icy pitchers by the wayside.

The villages were all much alike. Each hut or adobe house had an enclosure where goats, sheep and chickens were kept. The roads were fenced right through the villages and they used an ingenious method of fencing. They cut huge shoots of the organ cactus about equal lengths and stuck them in the ground so close that they touched one another. In a little while they took root and grew to enormous heights, many of them with small white flowers like daisies sticking ridiculously out at the top. All the owner of the fence had to do was to keep the straight shoots trimmed and tidy.

We rode through miles of these green lanes and then there would be a burst of open country with a magnificent view of the *sierras* on all sides. Each village could be located in the distance by its colonial church, built in Spanish-Moorish style with domes and massive walls. Most of the stone used was pinkish in colour and all along the valleys villages were marked by a patch of green with the pink walls of the church rising out of the trees. on the highway.

My house kept up a good pace but we had wasted so much time wandering around villages that it was dark before we reached Mitla. Luckily there was a moon and the road was clear. I had been told to expect to see the lights of Mitla long before I reached it and as I rode along in the moonlight I was puzzled and began to wonder if I could have missed the road. The valley stretched its shadowy way before me, but there were no lights. Suddenly my horse shied as we plunged into a lane made dark with the inevitable hedge of organ cactus. Presently a faint light showed in a *sorte*. Then we crossed the little *plaza* and stopped before the pillars of the old *hacienda* which is now the Hotel Mitla.

The *Señora* explained that there was no electric light. The machine had been taken to pieces for repairs and no one thought of putting it together again. However, she produced a lantern and a lamp and, having seen my horse tucked away in a comfortable stall with feed, I was shown into my room and told that supper would be ready in a few minutes. The room was whitewashed and the bed looked comfortable. I expected the usual bed-bugs, but by this time I was nonchalant about them. After a ten-hour ride nothing would keep me awake.

The food was a surprise. Well-flavoured soup, omelette with rice, tender mutton with fried potatoes, a delicious pie for dessert, all of it was beautifully served on fine linen. A small child waited on me. She was so fascinated by me that she could not keep her eyes off me for a moment. I was too hungry to worry about this scrutiny. When I at last fell into bed I just had time to notice the bed linen was very fine old linen with wonderful crocheted borders.

The next day I would out that the Hotel Mitla had been an *hacienda* belonging to the Quero family and that the *Señora* who ran the hotel was also a Quero, one of the last survivors. There seemed to be several aged relations bout the place and a *Señor* who was the proprietor of a small shop, call the Surprise, and the Post Office. The hotel seemed to be the centre of life in the village. Unfortunately the *Señora* seemed unable to forget that she came from a family of landowners. The *mozos* and the maids fairly skipped around when she appeared. There was also a large chromo of Franco hanging in one of the rooms, luckily not in mine. However, she was the best cook I had met in Mexico and when for breakfast she produced hot cakes and honey I decided that politics were a thing apart.

Mitla itself was the usual Zapotecan village, except for

ruins. I usually have no interest in ruins, but the Mitla ones are so well preserved and have such a collection of unique patterns called *grecos*, that I spent hours prowling around them copying the designs. The custodian was properly impressed and convinced I was going to write a history about them and I had not the heart to tell him I was merely planning tablecloths and bedspreads. Terry, whose phraseology makes his Guide to Mexico an abiding joy, in his 1909 edition describes the ruins thus:

'The scorching sun of southern Mexico has preserved the Mitla ruins so that they are in much the same condition today as they were when discovered by the Spaniards nearly four centuries ago. Their peculiar and elaborate style of ornamentation will give the traveller a fairly accurate idea of the degree of civilization reached by the mysterious people who dwelled in this favoured region centuries before the dawn of the present era. Government experts guard the ruins, make restorations, and check vandalism. Where the great stone lintels have been cracked by time or earthquakes, strong iron supports have been substituted. The efforts to preserve the ruins from obliteration are commendable. The contrast between the neatly-kept patio of the hotel, a-bloom with flowers, and the arid plain of powdery sand on which the ruins stand is striking—one typifying life, the other death.'

Terry mentions that the hotel is charming but that the sanitary arrangements are primitive. The moment I went into the toilet, an enormous barn-like room with a washbasin and a toilet perched up a flight of steps like some ancient throne, I realized that Terry had left his mark. Neatly written on a card tacked to the wall was the following notice:

'Please Do Not put newspapers or whatnots in the toilet. It decomposes easily and overflows. There is a receptacle at left to receive your offerings. Infringements of this are resented by the management. Please cooperate. Thank You.'

The neatly-kept patio was now overgrown with large shrubs and trees but it still had all its charm. I discovered a flat roof for sunbaths, which were necessary because of the intense cold out of the sun. I went around in a sweater at midday and wrapped a *sarape* around me morning and evening. I kept remaking on the unseasonable weather, being use to temperate Cuernavaca, and everyone politely agreed with me, although I discovered later that this was the usual Oaxaca weather. I had taken only one sweater with me, luckily a black one since I had to wear it everyday without a chance of washing it.

I liked Mitla so much I decided to stay there. I rode back to Oaxaca to collect my things and was greeted with open arms by Don Luis who enveloped me in a drunken embrace from which his *mozo* had to rescue me. Then we had a beer party and then I had to try on his new chaps. They were elegant chaps with silver decorations and fringes yards long and they fitted excellently except around the waistline. Then Don Luis, having been persuaded not to go riding in his maudlin state, insisted that I ride with him and the Governor when I was next in Oaxaca. We parted with many embraces and at the last minute he tried to do me down on the agreed price for his horse.

The ride back to Mitla was in a lorry . It took only three hours, but it was rougher than any horseback ride. I arrived again at the hotel, this time with typewriter and a change of clothes. The *Señora* had found me a horse for a quarter a day. I paid only 75 cents for my board and lodging.

The horse looked like a West Highland terrier. His face was hidden in his hair; his legs were so short his belly almost brushed the ground. He was snowy white and had a gay smile. I tried him out and found him about as exciting to ride as a steamroller. The *Señora* was so pleased with him that I decided to have him and he turned out to be adequate for long trips over the mountains. He was perfectly willing and would lumber happily over rocks and stones, and so long as I remembered to keep my feet well tucked up off the ground we got along very well.

I had a routine. There were no clocks in the house, although I imagine there may have been one in the Post Office, so I got up whenever I woke, which was usually when the sun first hit the patio. After a breakfast of eggs, coffee and milk, hot cakes and honey, I took a stroll on the roof. I enjoyed watching the women bringing their soaked corn to be ground into *masa*, the basis for most Indian food. It was pleasant to be able to watch them without being seen. There was a slight drawback to being the only foreigner in a community. The amount of attention I attracted was embarrassing. People ran to their doorways calling to their children to come quickly to look when I walked by. Everyone was friendly, but when the interest kept up for days I began to wonder if there was anything really peculiar about me. The *Señora* suggested it was because I was so blonde and at the same time so brown. She thought it was the saddest thing in the world that I had let myself get sunburned.

I wrote regularly every morning two thousand words and then, shivery with cold, ran up to the roof for a sunbath. I found a sheltered corner out of the gusts of wind that swept the valley; the sun poured down good and hot and by lunchtime I was warmed through. The lunch, always delicious, soup, chicken and vegetables, dessert, and after a cup of orange tea, the white monster would be brought round and I would go out for a long climb over the mountains. I always reckoned to be back before sundown because of the cold and then I would settle down to another two thousand words by the light of a candle, with a *sarape* round my shoulders.

After supper—soup again, hot *tortillas*, bread made out of corn meal, black beans, tender meat and salad—I would read for a while by the light of a strange lamp that flickered and glowed in an insane manner and then I would fall into bed and straightaway to sleep.

It was a great life. In some ways a perfect escapist life with no newspapers, no radio (I was thankful that the electric light was out), no time. I was alone all day long unless I wanted to chat with the *Señora* or one of the odd relations and I filled myself up every day with fresh air and glorious views. But after ten days or so I began to have a hankering after my house in Cuernavaca. How were Ella and Jack making out? How was Alhambra's figure? Had Chulita started barking all over again? Archie was due to have a holiday in Cuernavaca. It had been a swell holiday and I had done a lot of work but there was Christmas coming and I began to feel like going home.

Chapter 26
You Can Lead a Steamroller to Water

Behind the village there was a steep, high hill with a goat track leading to the top. The hill was only one of a range and the first time I climbed it I was surprised to find how large the range was. Instead of going down the other side, the hill stretched out in a plain surrounded by yet more hills which stretched away into an unending line of *sierras*.

By climbing to the top, a matter of a thousand feet, it was possible to see for miles across the valley where Mitla lies. The hill was so steep one got the impression of being in an airplane, and all the small tracks which were invisible from the ground showed up plainly. I found it a wonderful idea to climb the hill, plan my route, and to set off along it in the afternoon on my fine white steamroller. Distances were deceptive. I spotted a little village tucked away among the distant hills, only visible from the very top, and I decided to go there. The *Señora* told me it was twelve leagues away; the *mozo*, when he saw I wanted to go there, obligingly said it was only five leagues. I was not at all sure how much a league was anyway and decided to take a chance.

I also took a *sarape*, some food, and a bag of oranges, and explained that I might possibly stay overnight. The Señora told me to be sure to stay with some friends of hers who ran the village store, because she could not answer for anyone else in the village. She was doubtful about the whole expedition, and so were various charcoal burners and woodcutters I met in the mountains. They suggested they should escort me. I asked them why. Were there wild animals in the mountains.? No; there were deer, but no dangerous animals. It appeared that the only thing I might need protection from was charcoal burners and woodcutters. I thanked them very cordially for their kind offer of protection, but I declined it.

The steamroller could go on for ever. My horse from Oaxaca to Mitla had grown slightly tired after ten hours, while I was still fresh. But the steamroller plodded steadily on while I was aching in every bone. He had a way of planting down his forefeet with a sickening springless thud. I varied the agony by walking down the mountainsides, when the springlessness was most apparent. He was extremely w8illing, and when we occasionally came to an impasse of rocks to be scaled or ravines to be descended, he shut his white lashed eyes , waved the air with his forefeet, and plunged into space without a qualm.

The quiet of the mountains was beautiful. I have always hated noise, but I did not realize how much I appreciated quiet until I was wrapped up in it on the mountain tops. There was not a sound, no birds even. It pressed down all around like a soft, warm blanket. Every now and then I would stop the steamroller because the noise of his hoofs was shattering.

The village was farther than I thought, or else we had wandered among the mountain trails; but it was obvious that we could not reach it and return the same day. I decided it would be absurd to stay in the village when the whole *sierra* was mine. I found a camping place—a flat plateau sheltered on three sides by huge boulders with small scrubby trees growing out to form a roof. There was plenty of dry grass that the steamroller liked to eat. The only problem was how to get him a drink.

I have been brought up in the tradition that a horse

always comes first and it was unthinkable to watch the steamroller's tongue hanging out while I sucked oranges. I did what I had by this time learned to do in this country; I climbed to a high vantage point and looked around. There is little water at this time of year, but usually there are places at the foot of the hills where moisture seeps through and forms pools. The goats and sheep manage to find enough to keep them alive.

There was a glimmer of water away at the foot of the hill. I left my *sarape* and the saddle tucked under a boulder and laboriously led the steamroller down the mountainside. We skidded and slipped, but he did not complain, and at last we stood by the water. It was almost a small pond, and some sheep were drinking from it.

The steamroller looked at it and began to eat the green leaves off a shrub. I led him right up to it but he looked at me sadly. He was not thirsty.

I had tenderly led the steamroller one thousand feet down the mountain. I fairly whacked him up again.

The night was perfect. I could see little clouds of dust scuttering down the valley in the moonlight, but up in the mountains it was windless. I rolled myself in the *sarape* and with the saddle as a pillow I slept. I dreamed that the mountain was filled with Zapotecan warriors chatting in their soft language, and I awoke to find two charcoal burners and a woodcutter holding a long discussion in Zapotecan. They were shocked to think that I had spent a night alone in the mountains. Anything might have happened to me among the charcoal burners and woodcutters.

That day I spent wandering among the hills. I had lunch with some woodcutters, who exchanged *tamales* for oranges. I was not concerned about food because I can live for days on oranges. The steamroller was eating his head off and he did at last consent to take a drink when we reached a trickle that had formed into a small pool. The woodcutters and charcoal burners spoke Zapotecan with a smattering of Spanish. It is the most beautiful soft language, mostly sibilants with a great deal of the French 'j' sound. It is infinitely more beautiful than the harsh Náhuatl of the Aztecs and suits the less dominating, gentler people.

When I returned the *Señora* asked me how I had liked the village. I allowed her to think I had lost my way and was unable to find it. I could not explain to her that once up among the mountains the village did not seem important any more.

The small trip among the hills made me determined to ride to Tehuantepec whenever it was possible. The trip takes about six or seven days from Oaxaca and has to be made with a guide and proper provisions. Don Luis promised me that he would arrange everything for me whenever I wanted to go. I decided that when Archie could finish with his job we could celebrate by riding to Tehuantepec.

It seemed to me that in all probability I should have to stay in Mitla until Archie did finish his job and come down to join me. When I was in Oaxaca, in between visits to Mitla, I had cabled to Archie to ask him to send me fifty pesos. Knowing the complications of sending postal orders, I had said in the cable that he was to enclose a fifty pesos bill in an airmail letter to me at Mitla. It all sounded simple enough and I went to Mitla expecting to get the letter with the bill at any moment.

Hearing Archie's story afterwards did explain some of the difficulties, but the chief difficulty of all was Archie himself. The idea of sending a bill loose through the posts nearly killed him. He tried to send it through the Post Office, but the hours of the Mexican Post Office are strange and Archie ended by spending most of his waking hours waiting in lines and having the windows slam down in his face. When he was not doing that, he was writing me airmail letters which arrived every day at lunchtime by the one bus per day from Oaxaca to Mitla, telling me that he had not enclosed the fifty pesos because he was sure that the letter would never arrive. Finally he convinced himself that I was probably not really in Mitla at all and he wrote a letter explaining that it seemed utterly impossible to send me fifty pesos, that he was sure I could manage somehow and that he had done all he could. Then at the last minute he added a postscript—'Oh, to hell, I enclose a fifty pesos bill and chance it.'

So at long last I was able to pay my hotel bill and return to Mexico City.

The journey back by train seemed very long. The train crawled through the narrow gorges and each turn and bend showed more steep mountainsides covered with great clumps of organ cactus. After seven hours it was deadly boring. Sitting opposite to me a stout, fussy little Oaxaqueño who was going to visit relations in Mexico City. He was in a great state that we should not reach Puebla in time to catch the last bus for Mexico City, which left at 9.00 pm. It seemed doubtful that we should get to Puebla before ten, although we were scheduled to arrive at seven-thirty. If we missed the bus we had to spend the night in Puebla.

When we reached Tehuacan, the only other big town before Puebla, it was four-thirty and no one thought we could get to Puebla in under six hours. I suddenly had an idea. I asked when the last bus for Mexico City left Tehuacan. I was told at five o'clock. I said to the Oaxaqueño that we could leave the train right there and catch a bus to Mexico City. He was doubtful. He was sure there were no buses; if there were buses they would be full; it seemed an awful risk. And in any case, I think he was afraid that I was abducting him.

I left the train and picked up a cab to drive me to the bus station. The Oaxaqueño panted behind me. He was still convinced that I was leading him astray but he could not bear the idea of sitting any longer in the train which seemed to have gone to sleep in the station. The cab pulled up beside a second-class bus of the Flecha Roja line The driver assured us he was going to Mexico City. He was leaving right then.

The Oaxaqueño was so delighted he rushed straight off and bought five lottery tickets because he said obviously I was a lucky person.

We had a wonderful trip. Flecha Roja have comfortable seats and excellent engines and their drivers are supreme. The only drawback for most people is that they stop in the small villages and pick up passengers. They stop always near the local drinking den and women come up to the bus with the usual *tamales, enchiladas* and *quesadillas* and the men drink *pulque* and everyone eats. My Oaxaqueño was so grateful that I had made up his mind for him that he insisted on giving me huge tankards of draft black beer all along the line. We whizzed through Puebla at seven-thirty (the train was three hours behind time) and arrived in Mexico City at ten o'clock, a journey of just over five hours. We got to Mexico City before the train got to Puebla. The whole trip from Oaxaca had taken sixteen hours.

It was good to be back in Cuernavaca. Cuernavaca

looked sophisticated and overloaded with colour after Oaxaca, but the sun was hot and everything looked green and fresh. I arrived for lunch and found Ella alone; Jack had just left for Mexico City. Ella was pleased to see me for several reasons. The ants had made frightful forays against the plants and Ella was in agony every time a leaf was eaten; Alhambra had missed me and had decided that she might as well go back to her original owners and Ella felt that she must keep her at all costs until I got back; Biscuit, whom we had sent to stay in the country, where he had more room to stretch his long legs, had turned up again. Also the Harpies and the Vultures had been doing their little act while I was away, taking the chance to do as much carrion-snatching as they could.

Ella had always lived in a large city among reasonably civilized people and she had had no experience of the back-biting that goes on in small communities. I have always lived either so far in the country that there was no one else around, or else in or near villages and I thought nothing much in the way of really dirty gossip could surprise me. But Mexico foreign colonies certainly topped any place I have ever been. I swear the Harpies sat up all night thinking out schemes to start stories about their dearest friends. The Vultures were just scavengers who flapped around after the pieces. It seemed to me that behind it all was fear, fear of losing possessions or power, fear of other people's happiness, fear of that brooding, waiting silence of Mexico.

After a year and a half in Mexico I came to the conclusion that it is nonsense to generalise about Mexico. There are several Mexicos. There is the Mexico that belongs to the Indians, the wide plains, the sweeping hills, the deep forests and jungles, with the rhythm of turkeys gobbling, the slapping of *tortillas*, *chirimeros* plaintively piping, drums beating. There is the Mexico of the towns, modern buildings, paved streets, slick Mexican business men, slicker government officials, automobiles and more automobiles. There is the Mexico of the foreign colonies, a cheap place to live where the foreigners can get all their comforts and feel superior in a superb climate, although sometimes the climate lets them down and their superiority clouds occasionally. There is the Mexico of the guide books, a land of gay *sombreros*, fascinating women, handsome men, continually dancing and playing guitars, tossing around flowers and with nothing more to do in life than to entertain the tourists.

Everyone can invent his own idea of Mexico. The Mexican people have one common aim They want to be free—in the sense that they want to feel themselves a separate entity, not just a satellite of the United States— and they consider themselves as good as any other people on the American continent. Many foreigners find this surprising, which is one of the reasons that Mexicans are not crazy about foreigners.

Sometimes one meets an understanding foreigner. My first afternoon back in Cuernavaca was made perfect by the arrival of a small elderly lady on my porch. I stared at her and she said in a soft Irish brogue:

'You don't remember me? I was in Barcelona. "*La Suegra*", they used to call me.'

Of course I remembered her. La Suegra, the mother-in-law, she was called because her son-in-law was the Hitler-exiled Prince Hubertus zu Loewenstein who visited Republican Spain as a Catholic and who was a firm supporter of the Republican cause. But she was remembered better as the dauntless little old lady who gave our *ánimo* or spirit to the Spaniards in air-raids; who shook her fist at the German planes which bombed Barcelona for seventy hours consecutively including, including blow up the house next to her hotel and flinging her on to the floor among the collapsed ceiling; who had to be restrained from visiting the blood donation centre too frequently; who stayed on in Barcelona because she felt that with her knowledge of languages she could be helpful.

'How did you get my address?' I asked, when we had settled La Suegra on the terrace with tea. 'How did you know I was in Mexico?'

That was quite a story. On my way to Oaxaca I had spent a night in Puebla. I had casually met an American girl in the bus and we decided to share a room in a hotel to save expenses. We had dinner together, went to bed and I crept away at six in the morning to get the train to Oaxaca. In conversation over dinner, I mentioned that I had been in Spain and she told me that she had met a Dutch woman who had also been in Spain during the Spanish war and that she would be seeing this person again. I said casually to give her my address in Cuernavaca, I was always pleased to see anyone who had been in Spain. I left my address with the American girl, caught my train and did not give the matter another thought.

The result was that La Suegra walked in to see us.

Ella and I both felt fine after La Suegra had gone, promising to come back and to stay in Cuernavaca for some months. La Suegra has that effect on people. She is so quiet and so charming and with such an indomitable spirit that she gives '*ánimo*' to everyone, even without the air-raids. Ella and I had sunk into apathy about getting anything done for Spanish refugees: La Suegra admitted the difficulties but she refused to admit defeat. La Suegra will probably get to work and Ella and I will find ourselves running children's colonies, relief work or organizing collective farms. I have tremendous faith in La Suegra. So has everyone who meets her.

She said about Mexico:

'Mexico is a wonderful country, but there is so much to *do* here. Everywhere I look I see things to do, but perhaps it is hard to get things done.

Chapter 27
Stocktaking

Christmas descended upon us with a rush. Christmas is always a problem in foreign countries. It seems absurd to stick doggedly to the rigid British Christmas traditions in the blazing sun. Archie and I had privately decided to give Christmas a miss this year but our friends decided otherwise. Ella and Jack wanted some sort of celebration, friends from Mexico City decided to visit us; Archie got five days off and felt like enjoying himself.

George and Mary, our geese, who were boarded out, were too old for a Christmas meal, but we did a deal over them for three ducks. Geroge and Mary were to be allowed another chance to raise a family in the spring and we were to have a gosling if it all went well. I have never eaten sufficient duck. I have often thought of cooking a duck and just eating it by myself instead of toying with the polite slices of breast which usually come my way. Somehow I have never got as far as cooking and eating a duck, but this Christmas I decided that for once I would have enough duck to eat.

We compromised over a Christmas tree. We found a strange kind of cactus with spiky leaves and spiky pink flowers and we stuck it in a pot and decorated it with orthodox Christmas-tree decorations. It looked perfectly idiotic, but perfectly grand. We put around it our joint collection of little animals, clay figures, the usual Mexican Christmas figures of saints wearing *sombreros*. The Indians think of halos as a kind of hat and they always model saints with large sombreros on the backs of their heads. The tree looked very gay and our back porch was decorated with flowers.

I gave Archie an oven for a Christmas present. That meant that he could have plenty of cookies and pies. He was mysterious about his present for me. He said he would bring it with him when he came down. He meant to arrive on Christmas morning.

Ella was not sure what Jack might be doing over Christmas, although she threatened to leave him if he did not show up. Jack was commuting between Cuernavaca and a remote village in the interior where some friends of his were getting him to negotiate the sale of a mine for them. These friends occasionally came to visit Don Santiago, as they called Jack, and if Jack was away, Ella and I would entertain them. They were charming young men, brothers, who lived in this tiny village where the only communications were by bus and then six hours on horseback. One of them lamented that the village had no radio. If he and his brother managed to put the mining deal through, they intended to buy a radio, if they would get one that worked on batteries without electricity, and an oil stove for their mother. They questioned us closely about world events, and it was difficult to give them much idea, because we did not know where to start. We were talking about Spain and they were astonished to learn that Spaniards spoke the same language as they did. They had thought that England was in the United States: that is a frequent mistake among Indians—or perhaps they are just ahead of history. It was curious to talk to two such intelligent people with so little of the rudimentary knowledge that we had. The elder brother was convinced that a radio would make a great difference to their outlook.

Jack was negotiating the sale of their mercury mines.

They had a buyer, but he was a foreigner and they realized that they stood no chance in a deal with an unscrupulous foreigner, and it seemed that many foreigners were unscrupulous. So they wanted Don Santiago to put the deal through for them. They trusted him implicitly and they felt it was worth paying him a commission and his expenses rather than trusting to the foreigner, who might or might not try to swindle them. Jack was pleased to take it over. He was fond of the two boys and he was glad to have something to do while he was waiting for the final arrangements to be made about his job on the cattle ranch.

Arranging any kind of a job in Mexico took time. Before the elections there were no jobs—everyone was in a state of jitters and the Mexicans were taking no chances in expanding their businesses and foreign capital was not coming in. Jack was essentially a miner: he loved the excitements and he did not mind discomfort and hard work. To him mining was romantic. He grew as lyrical over a sample of rock as Ella and I over a plant in the garden. While Ella and I would go into raptures over a new batch of preserves, Jack would almost croon over a job of examining samples of rock. But Jack realized that mining needed capital and there was no capital. It was clear that with the United States piling up armaments, the Mexican mining industry would boom, but it was a question of hanging on. Ella and Jack could not hang on indefinitely. The job on the *rancho* was the first piece of luck which had come their way in a long while. The ranch was in mining country, and we had visions of Jack, about to lasso a galloping steer, suddenly leaping from his horse and scratching madly in the earth to get samples. It seemed probable that Jack's cattle would be driven underground.

Jack's idea of commuting was to leave Cuernavaca at the

crack of dawn, take a bus as far as he could, and then walk for five or six hours until he reached the village where his friends lived. He would drop in to see us for a night and then disappear for a few days and as suddenly turn up again, unshaven and dusty, to assure us that he could only stay a few hours—he had to get to Mexico City. Ella and I decided that we might as well consider ourselves *solteras* and have done with it. But we kept that to ourselves. Two houses near ours were tenanted by lone Mexican husbands—their wives were staying in Mexico City—and they considered themselves extremely *solteros*. Whenever they met us they assured us that life was not meant to be like that. One was not meant to live alone, they would suggest wistfully.

Archie and I were glad that Ella and Jack had some prospects of a settled existence, even if it were in a tree. We were feeling so fine that Christmas seemed a celebration of our successful life in Mexico. We considered that we had been extremely successful, although many people might not agree with us.

We arrived eighteen months before with nothing but 250 dollars and our health. In eighteen months we had achieved plenty and, most important, we had enjoyed the time spent in achieving it. Archie had one bad spell working on *The Good Neighbour*, but he found that it was worth it because he made money on it and he appreciated his life in Cuernavaca far more. Archie enjoyed teaching, which he thinks is a worthwhile job; we enjoyed making home out of the two little houses we had lived in; we enjoyed painting up furniture and making things for the house. I had written an novel, published in England, and three-quarters of this book, and while I do not enjoy writing, I do not find it a great hardship. Archie finally got a newspaper job, which is not his idea of heaven, but at least it is work which he does well and which pays well. Archie does not feel he will spend the rest of his life working in Mexico City, but he does enjoy the sensation of building up a bank account which will give us a feeling of security. We neither of us mind having little money, but we both like to have a few dollars in case of emergency. There is always the possibility that we might want to return to Europe. At the moment we prefer Mexico, but there might be eventualities which call us back to Spain or to England. We both like to feel that we have the money in case there is work for us there.

I sometimes smile when I think of my early upbringing. I was raised among the 'landed gentry', that class which was badly shaken by the last war and which will probably not survive this war. America has been spared the landed gentry as understood in England. In their day the landed gentry had their uses, but they died so long ago and would not realize it. I had the most wonderful childhood in the country with ponies, horses, sailing boats, even a cottage of my very own. Just before my thirteenth birthday someone inquired of me what I was going to ask for.

'You seem to have almost everything,' she suggested.

I thought for a while. I agreed that I really had everyting that anyone could want.

'Well,' I said, 'I could always do with another horse.'

I could always do with another horse. Luckily I seem to ber up without a horse at all, but there is no doubt that I could always do with one. I was thrilled to find tht I could afford to hire the little brown horse occasionally. I even inspired Ella.

Ella did not know anything at all about horses, but she agreed with me that if she could manage to ride one it would widen her horizon, if nothing else. She had to ride side-saddle and side-saddles were not available, so I suggested she try sitting sideways on an ordinary saddle, the way the Mexican women ride to market. I did not quite realize what a tremendous step it was for Ella to ride a horse. I find riding much easier and more comfortable than walking.

Ella climbed on the horse's back and I led him until we reached a quiet lane. Then I walked away, leaving Ella to ride the horse.

I do not know which was the more horrified. Ella or the horse. He was convinced that his only hope was to stay right by me so he followed me with an agonized look in his eye while Ella clutched the reins and looked as if she were in an earthquake. Then suddenly she realized that everything was fine. There she was, sitting up on the horse, and there was the horse walking along, just like a horse. She gathered up the reins and proceeded to ride. After a while I heard her say:

'Now listen, I want you to go that way, and what I say goes around here.'

Presently she was saying, 'Come on now, hurry, will you?' Then to me: 'What do you do when you want him to go fast?'

The next day Ella rode seven miles while the dogs and I ran behind.

Archie came down unexpectedly from Mexico City on Christmas Eve. Jack had arrived fifteen minutes before and I was thinking of scratching Ella's eyes out when Archie appeared and I felt how wonderful it was that Jack had been able to make it after all.

Christmas Day was brilliantly sunny and we all felt gay. Archie mysteriously disappeared after breakfast for a while and came back with a red face and shining eyes. He was leading horse. A nice little brown horse, a horse which had won all the races in the penitentiary and which I had hired for 45 cents and hour.

'His name is Golondrino,' said Archie. 'So it says on his papers. I have just bought him for you.'

So I have a horse, too.

ALSO AVAILABLE FROM THE CLAPTON PRESS

MY HOUSE IN MALAGA by Sir Peter Chalmers Mitchell
While most ex-pats fled to Gibraltar in 1936, Sir Peter stayed on to protect his house and servants from the rebels. He ended up in prison for sheltering Arthur Koestler from Franco's rabid head of propaganda, who had threatened to 'shoot him like a dog'.

BRITISH WOMEN AND THE SPANISH CIVIL WAR by Angela Jackson — 2020 Edition
Angela Jackson's classic examination of the interaction between British women and the war in Spain, through their own oral and written narratives. Revised and updated for this new edition.

BOADILLA by Esmond Romilly
The nephew that Winston Churchill disowned describes his experiences fighting with the International Brigade to defend the Spanish Republic. Written on his honeymoon in France after he eloped with Jessica Mitford.

SOME STILL LIVE by F.G. Tinker Jr.
Frank Tinker was a US pilot who signed up with the Republican forces because he didn't like Mussolini. He was also attracted by the prospect of adventure and a generous pay cheque. This is an account of his experiences in Spain.

SPANISH PORTRAIT by Elizabeth Lake
A brutally honest, semi-autobiographical novel set in San Sebastián and Madrid between 1934 and 1936, portraying a frantic love affair against a background of confusion and apprehension as Spain drifted inexorably towards civil war.

MARGUERITE REILLY by Elizabeth Lake
First published in 1946, Marguerite Reilly is the fictionalised story of four generations of Irish immigrants struggling to make good in the Victorian and post-Victorian era, from the days of the Great Hunger up to the end of the second world war. Harrowing at times but always entertaining, this is a must-read for anyone with Anglo-Irish heritage.

ALSO AVAILABLE FROM THE CLAPTON PRESS

NEVER MORE ALIVE: INSIDE THE SPANISH REPUBLIC by Kate Mangan, with a Preface by Paul Preston
When her lover, Jan Kurzke, made his way to Spain to join the International Brigade in 1936, Kate Mangan went after him. She ended up working with Constancia de la Mora in the Republic's Press Office, where she met a host of characters including WH Auden, Stephen Spender, Ernest Hemingway, Robert Capa, Gerda Taro, Walter Reuter and many more. When Jan was seriously injured she visited him in hospital, helped him across the border to France and left him with friends in Paris so she could return to her job in Valencia.

THE GOOD COMRADE, MEMOIRS OF AN INTERNATIONAL BRIGADER by Jan Kurzke, with an Introduction by Richard Baxell
Jan Kurzke was a left-wing artist who fled Nazi Germany in the early 1930s and tramped round the south of Spain, witnessing first-hand the poverty of the rural population, later moving to England where he met Kate Mangan. When the Spanish civil war broke out in 1936, Jan went back and joined the International Brigade, while Kate followed shortly after, working for the Republican press office. Many of his fellow volunteers died in the savage battles on the outskirts of Madrid and Jan himself was seriously wounded at Boadilla, nearly losing his leg. This is his memoir, a companion volume to *Never More Alive*.

IN PLACE OF SPLENDOUR: THE AUTOBIOGRAPHY OF A SPANISH WOMAN by Constancia de la Mora, with a foreword by Soledad Fox Maura
Constancia de la Mora was the grand-daughter of Antonio Maura, who had served under Alfonso XIII as Prime Minister. She was one of the first women to obtain a divorce under the fledgling Spanish Republic. During the civil war she became a key figure in the Republic's International Press Office, moving to the USA and Mexico after the war was lost. This is her remarkable memoir, with a detailed history of the build-up to the conflict.

ALSO AVAILABLE FROM THE CLAPTON PRESS

**NEVER MORE ALIVE: INSIDE THE SPANISH REPUBLIC
by Kate Mangan, with a Preface by Paul Preston**
When her lover, Jan Kurzke, joined the International Brigade in 1936, Kate Mangan followed him to Spain. She found a job with the Republican Press Office, meeting a host of characters including Auden, Spender, Hemingway, Robert Capa, Gerda Taro, Walter Reuter and many more. When Jan was seriously injured she helped him across the border to France and left him with friends in Paris so she could return to her job in Valencia.

**THE GOOD COMRADE, MEMOIRS OF AN INTERNATIONAL BRIGADER
by Jan Kurzke, with an Introduction by Richard Baxell**
Jan Kurzke was an artist who fled Nazi Germany in the early 1930s and tramped round Spain, witnessing first-hand the poverty of the rural population. When the civil war broke out in 1936, Jan joined the International Brigade. Many of his fellow volunteers died in the battle for Madrid and Jan himself was seriously wounded at Boadilla, nearly losing a leg. This is his memoir, a companion volume to *Never More Alive*.

**IN PLACE OF SPLENDOUR: THE AUTOBIOGRAPHY OF A SPANISH WOMAN by Constancia de la Mora,
with a foreword by Soledad Fox Maura**
Constancia de la Mora was the rebellious grand-daughter of Antonio Maura, who had served under Alfonso XIII as Prime Minister. She was one of the first women to obtain a divorce under the fledgling Spanish Republic. During the civil war ran the Republican Press Office. This is her remarkable memoir, with a detailed history of the build-up to the conflict.

**BEHIND THE SPANISH BARRICADES
by John Langdon-Davies, with a Prologue by Paul Preston**
First published in 1936, *Behind the Spanish Barricades* chronicles the early months of the Spanish Civil War through the eyes of a seasoned journalist well acquainted with Spanish and Catalan cultures. Arriving on a second-hand motorbike, he experiences the exuberant atmosphere in Barcelona during its short-lived proletarian revolution, as well as the horrors of war as he visits Toledo during the siege of the Alcázar.

ALSO AVAILABLE FROM THE CLAPTON PRESS

FIRING A SHOT FOR FREEDOM: THE MEMOIRS OF FRIDA STEWART with a Foreword and Afterword by Angela Jackson
Frida Stewart drove an ambulance to Murcia to help the Spanish Republic and visited the front in Madrid. During the Second World War she was arrested by the Gestapo in Paris and escaped from her internment camp with help from the French Resistance, returning to London where she worked with General de Gaulle. This is her previously unpublished memoir.

STRUGGLE FOR THE SPANISH SOUL & SPAIN IN THE POST-WAR WORLD by Arturo and Ilsa Barea, with Introduction by William Chislett.
Arturo and Ilsa Barea worked for the Spanish Republic's Press and Censorship office and later sought refuge in the UK. These two essays, both written during the Second World War, called on the democracies of Europe to unseat Franco; both fell on deaf ears. Together the two essays present a horrific picture of the early years of the dictatorship., which endured until 1975.

THE FIGHTER FELL IN LOVE: A SPANISH CIVIL WAR MEMOIR by James R Jump, with a Foreword by Paul Preston and a Preface by Jack Jones
Aged twenty-one, James R Jump went to Spain to join the International Brigade. This previously unpublished memoir, based on his diaries, brings back to life his time in Spain and the tragic course of the war he took part in, while the accompanying poems reflect the intense emotions sparked by his experience.

SINGLE TO SPAIN & ESCAPE FROM DISASTER by Keith Scott Watson
The author was one of the first British volunteers to join the International Brigades; within a couple of months most of the British in his battalion were dead and he had been chased out of Spain as a deserter. He soon returned to Spain and was one of the first journalists on the spot to report on the bombing of Guernica in April 1937. *Single to Spain* is his memoir of his experiences in the siege of Madrid, first published in 1937. *Escape from Disaster* is his report on the fall of Barcelona and his desperate dash for the border in January 1939.

ALSO AVAILABLE FROM THE CLAPTON PRESS
BY THE SAME AUTHOR

HOTEL IN SPAIN by Nancy Johnstone
Bored with life in London, Nancy and Archie Johnstone left their jobs and moved to the Costa Brava in 1934 to build and run their own hotel. It sounded like a recipe for disaster but within twelve months Tossa de Mar became the destination of choice for a vibrant group of international writers and artists. *Hotel in Spain* is a light-hearted account of their ups and downs before the Civil War erupted and darkness descended.

HOTEL IN FLIGHT by Nancy Johnstone
After declining the Royal Navy's offer to rescue them from Tossa de Mar as civil war erupts across Spain, the Johnstones decide to convert their hotel into a refuge for displaced children, eventually escorting their "colony" across the border into France, as Franco's mercenary army advanced on Barcelona. In this sequel to *Hotel in Spain*, Nancy Johnstone continues their story and provides a fascinating record of their experiences in wartime Spain, including their final terrifying dash for the border.

www.theclaptonpress.com

CPSIA information can be obtained
at www.ICGtesting.com
Printed in the USA
LVHW080552230223
740172LV00016B/1245